FABULOUS FOOD

FOR FAMILY AND FRIENDS

Healthy Menus for Entertaining With Style

▼

Cheryl Thomas Caviness, D.T.R.

This book was
Designed by Bill Kirstein
Photography by Meylan Thoresen
Type set: 11/12 Cheltenham Book

Printed in U.S.A.

Library of Congress Cataloging-in-Publication Data
Caviness, Cheryl Thomas, 1962-
    For family and friends: vegetarian menus for
entertaining with style / Cheryl Thomas Caviness.
        p.   cm.
    1. Vegetarian cookery.   I. Title.
TX837.C35   1990   90-8355
641.5'636—dc20   CIP

ISBN 0-8280-0567-2

About the Photographs

   A "food shot" is not every photographer's favorite as-signment. But Meylan Thoresen, who is responsible for all the photographs in this book, considers culinary photography one of his specialties. Working closely with author Cheryl Caviness, who prepared every item of food in the pictures, Meylan served as both food stylist and photographer. Most of the shots were made on location, using real homes and natural outdoor settings.

   Meylan is the owner of The Photo Department, a commercial photography studio in Portland, Oregon, that specializes in advertising, still-life, illustration, editorial, and culinary photography.

Dedication

To my precious daughter,

Cherié Cara-Mae.

Jesus made you special,

and may you always dedicate your life

to Him.

Acknowledgments

With much love to my husband, Merrill, and children, Kenneth Dwight and Cherié Cara-Mae, who constantly encouraged me and understood my busy schedule. With love and appreciation to my mother, Carol, my mother-in-law, Alice, my sister-in-law, Jolene, and my Aunt Barbara for their hours of untiring effort, and to all my family and friends who gave me encouragement and ideas. A special thank you to Clinton Wall, R.D., for his encouragement and assistance in the initial planning of this book.

Thank you to everyone who lent dishes and props for the photos in this book, especially Beaver Creek Antique Mall, and Carol Mohler of Carol and Company, both of Hagerstown, Maryland.

And to the owners of homes who allowed us to photograph the menus in beautiful settings, my heartfelt gratitude. Jeffrey C. Kline, Martha J. and Hugh J. Talton, and Diane and Robert L. Elder, your kindness and hospitality will long be remembered and appreciated.

Introduction

Today, everyone would like to be slim, energetic, healthy, and happy. And we're learning to eat in ways that will help us stay that way. So today's menus have to be more than delicious and attractive. To keep us fit, we want meals that are light in cholesterol, low in fat, and light in sodium and processed sugar. And because of our busy lifestyles, they have to be quick and easy to prepare as well.

This book meets these requirements by providing 18 complete, heart-healthy menus for all occasions, menus that take the guesswork out of planning healthy meals. Included are more than 130 recipes, developed especially for this book. Each recipe has been thoroughly kitchen-tested. And they've been tried out on friends and family, large groups and small. They've been sampled by those who "eat to live," as well as by those who "live to eat," and pronounced delicious by both.

Each menu includes computer-analyzed nutrition information on the amounts of calories, protein, fat, cholesterol, sodium, and seven other major nutrients, along with the percentage of the United States recommended daily allowances, where applicable. Also included for each complete menu are the six diabetic exchange lists, to help you when you cook for those with special dietary needs, such as low-fat or diabetic diets. A chart at the end of the book lists the same information by recipe. All of these features are designed to help you cook and eat the healthiest meals possible, even when you're entertaining in style.

These recipes meet the American Heart Association's dietary recommendations and the American Cancer Society's dietary guidelines. These delicious meals contain little or no cholesterol, and eliminate fat-saturated, high-cholesterol items such as meat.

The ideas behind this book are hardly new. God's original diet for man is found in Genesis 1:29, "Behold, I have given you every herb bearing seed, which is upon the face of all the earth, and every tree, in the which is the fruit of a tree yielding seed; to you it shall be for meat." And after sin God extended this diet in Genesis 3:18, ". . . and thou shalt eat the herb of the field."

This book uses these original all-natural ingredients, such as fruits, vegetables, grains, nuts, and seeds, and carefully combines them to provide attractive, easy-to-prepare, properly balanced, heart-healthy meals that are fun to prepare, beautiful to look at, and delicious to eat.

Adventists, who believe strongly in the importance of a healthy lifestyle, recognize this book as an example of an ideal vegetarian dietary regime. Each recipe has dietary options for lacto-ovo vegetarians (who include milk and egg products in their diets) and vegan vegetarians (who leave out milk and egg products). So *you* can decide how you want to cook and eat.

Even if you've never tried either vegetarian or heart-healthy cooking before, you'll love these easy, delicious, and nutritious menus for any occasion, from light soup and salad luncheons, to a hearty La Fiesta Grande Buffet. And you'll appreciate the whole section packed full of delightfully delicious desserts to add to any meal you choose.

When you serve these meals to your family or guests, you'll have the extra pleasure of knowing you're contributing to their well-being. This book will provide you with mouth-watering, eye-appealing, nutritionally balanced vegetarian meals that can begin a lifetime of living well for your family and your guests.

Nutritional Goals of This Book

The menus and recipes in this cookbook are designed to aid in the prevention of heart and blood disease and cancer, which are major causes of death. To achieve this, the following guidelines have been established:

Menus contain decreased amounts of cholesterol and fat.

A variety of plant foods has been used for every menu. The proper amounts of protein and other nutrients can thus be assured without meat in the diet, which greatly lowers dietary cholesterol and fat.

Menus contain no more than one-fourth egg per serving. Egg yolks have been almost entirely omitted to lower cholesterol. (Incidentally, don't feel guilty about "wasting good food" when you discard egg yolks. Think of it the same way you would think of trimming excess fat when preparing meat.) They are replaced with egg whites, in the dairy option recipes, or tofu, in the nondairy option recipes. Every recipe contains nondairy options, using replacements for dairy products that taste surprisingly delicious. Don't be afraid to try leaving out dairy products by using the nondairy variations found after the last menu in the book. These options eliminate all cholesterol in each menu.

Oil and margarine are used in place of shortening and butter to decrease saturated fats and cholesterol, and to increase polyunsaturated fats, which have been found to lower cholesterol and triglycerides, which helps prevent heart disease. (If you're following a therapeutic low-cholesterol or low-fat diet, be sure to delete oils and margarine whenever they are included as optional ingredients.) Nutrition information is based on the low-fat options and low-sodium options. Optional ingredients are not included in nutrient calculations.

When you shop for margarine, read the labels. Look for a product that lists a liquid vegetable oil as its first ingredient (such as corn, soy, safflower, etc.) rather than a hydrogenated vegetable oil. It will have less saturated fat and increased amounts of polyunsaturated fat, which has been found to decrease risks of heart disease.

When oil is called for in recipes, try using canola oil or olive oil. Both work well in salad dressing, tomato-based foods, etc. (Olive oil has a tendency to dominate lightly flavored foods.) Both canola oil and olive oil are high in monounsaturated fats, which may aid in lowering cholesterol. Other oils to consider are corn oil, safflower oil, and soy oil.

These recipes contain no refined sugar. It is replaced with honey, which in its unprocessed raw state is a fructose sugar, which is quicker and easier to digest. Molasses and fruit juices are also used as sweeteners.

Recipes feature high-fiber foods. Refined foods are replaced with foods in their natural state, such as whole-wheat flour, whole grain rice, legumes, vegetables, fruits, nuts, and seeds.

The menus include low-cholesterol gourmet desserts made with unrefined sweeteners, whole-grain flours, fresh fruits, etc., that are combined to be delicious, attractive, and easy to prepare.

Baking soda and baking powder are deleted in every recipe to prevent high amounts of aluminum residue in the body and to prevent irritation to the stomach. "The question of using baking powder or soda involves some very sophisticated chemistry. However, since soda (all baking powders contain it) destroys vitamins in food in which it is used and because of the chemical residues from the use of baking powder in cooking, we have sought acceptable alternatives" (R. S. Harris, *Evaluation of Food Processing*, p. 477).

Certain seasonings have been found to irritate some people's digestive systems. Therefore, the variation section at the end of the book provides nonirritating alternates to such seasonings as chili powder and cinnamon. Black pepper has been omitted entirely. Vinegar has been replaced with lemon juice.

Nutrition information is based on Nutritionist III, a computer program designed for nutritional diet analyses, produced by N-Squared Computing. In analyzing these recipes these guidelines were followed:

Nutrition information is calculated on one serving of each recipe listed in the menu outline, unless otherwise indicated in the recipe. Serving sizes are based on the total amount of food divided by the largest serving, unless otherwise stated. For example, in "serves 8, makes 2 cups," the serving size would be based on 8 ¼-cup servings.

When ingredients are stated as "optional" or "to taste," they have been deleted from the nutrition information owing to the difficulty in calculating exact amounts used in each individual case.

When options are given for amounts of ingredients (example, ½ to ¾ cup) the nutrition information is based on the smallest amount given.

If you're following a therapeutic diet, be sure to read this entire section carefully for guidelines to help you follow the lowest cholesterol, lowest fat, lowest sodium, and lowest sugar diets possible in these recipes.

Foreword

It is so refreshing to see the mind of a trained nutritionist comprehend the nutritional value of foods in the marketplace and bring them together in menus that are so appealing, delicious, and satisfying. We appreciate the author's skill of masterminding uniquely designed menus that provide beauty on the dining table and balance in nutrition.

As you prepare each recipe, let it be an experience of learning and inspiration that you can build on. Let your mind be creative and imaginative. The rewards will be boundless and thrilling, teaching children to do likewise.

Wise, advanced planning of the recipes in this book results in relative ease of preparation prior to eating time and optimum nutritional value.

Common foods simply prepared offer the best in nutrition and ultimately give lasting health; they provide caring for one's self without the experience of sickness.

The option of providing a dietary plan including dairy products—or their total absence, as well as less salt, sugar, and fat—will meet the personal tastes and health preferences of those who care to be more precise in all their eating habits. Science does support the conclusion that a pure balanced vegetarian diet adds years to a useful and enjoyable life.

There is reason to believe that today's generation can live to the allotted scriptural 70 years by following the rules of good nutrition, physical exercise, and productive thinking.

Let us trust in God and listen to His Spirit to gain generous insights into preparing all our meals for positive health and full enjoyment in atmosphere and elegant beauty.

Clinton A. Wall, R.D.
Director/Consultant
Adventist Food Service

CONTENTS

How to Get Started

A Peek Into Cheryl's Pantry

When I conduct cooking classes or talk to people about learning to cook healthy meals, one question inevitably comes up. "How in the world do I get started?" people ask. They tell me they read recipe books with words like "tofu," and "Do-Pep" and "tahini," and they get confused. Those words are in this book, too, and some others that may also be new to you. If that's the case, I invite you to take a peek inside my pantry and refrigerator. Naturally, you won't rush out and buy all these things at once, but gradually, as you develop your own healthful cooking style, they'll become a part of your pantry, too. Here's what you'll find on my shelves:

GRAINS

Rolled oats (oatmeal). Buy either the regular or quick-cooking kind.

Oat bran. This is available at many grocery stores and health food stores.

Cornmeal. Whole grain is best, but most grocers sell only cornmeal that has the bran and germ removed. I like to use yellow cornmeal for the nice coloring it gives to food, but white cornmeal is equally nutritious.

Corn tortillas, soft and uncooked. These may be purchased in the refrigerator or freezer section of the supermarket. They keep well when frozen.

Popcorn. White hull-less is my favorite kind.

Rice. Buy whole-grain brown rice. Long-grain brown rice will give you lighter, fluffier cooked rice dishes.

Millet. Whole millet can be found in health food stores. It has much the same flavor as rice, but it is somehow refreshingly different.

Wheat flour. I keep all flours in the freezer to preserve their freshness and gluten content. Old flour is the cause of many batches of poor bread. (Be sure to bring the flour to room temperature before using it in baking.) The best flour for breadmaking is milled just before use. If you plan to do a lot of breadmaking, consider investing in an electric home mill, such as the Bosch.

I use whole-wheat flour for most of my baking. It has higher amounts of fiber and nutrients than white flour. However, whole-wheat flour can make yeast-raised baked goods heavy because it has a lower gluten concentration than white flour. Gluten is the protein portion of the wheat. It makes the dough elastic and easy to handle, and allows the bread to rise nicely and maintain its shape. You can get light, delectable whole-wheat baked goods by adding a small amount of a special whole-wheat high-gluten flour, also called Do-Pep, to your recipes. Look for Do-Pep, or a similar whole-wheat product with at least 75 percent gluten, in your health food store.

For breadmaking, look for a high-protein "hard" wheat flour. Hard wheat has a higher gluten content for lighter raised baked goods. For pastry or other non-yeast baked products, choose an all-purpose or "soft" wheat flour. Its lower gluten content produces a more tender pastry.

Enriched unbleached white flour. It's good to keep this on hand. You'll want to combine it with whole-wheat flour in some recipes.

Wheat germ. This product is the heart of the wheat and adds a nice nutty flavor to many recipes. It is available raw or toasted. Toasted wheat germ has a longer shelf life and a nuttier flavor, but less nutrients than the raw. Be sure to store raw wheat germ in the freezer to maintain freshness.

Pasta. The nutritional analysis for the recipes in this book is based on the standard white noodle. If you need an even higher fiber diet, replace white noodles with whole-wheat pasta. The pastas used in the book are linguini, a long noodle that looks like flattened spaghetti, and wide lasagna noodles.

NUTS AND SEEDS

You can buy nuts and seeds raw and roast them yourself if you like. Roast them in a shallow pan in a 300° F oven. Most nuts and seeds can be found at the grocery store or health food store. Investigate your local co-op for a less expensive source. Store large quantities of nuts and seeds in the freezer to preserve freshness.

Pecans, raw, chopped.
Almonds, raw, slivered and sliced.
Cashews, unsalted, roasted.
Peanut butter. Be a label-reader. Buy peanut butter that lists only peanuts and salt on the label, and has no added oils, sweeteners, or preservatives. This may be harder to find than you think. Grocery stores will usually carry at least one such brand. Adams and Smuckers both make an additive-free peanut butter. Of course, you can also make your own peanut butter by putting peanuts through a grinder attachment on your food processor. Natural peanut butter, whether homemade or bought in a store, will sometimes separate, leaving the oil on the top. That's why I keep unopened jars of peanut butter upside down on my pantry shelf until I am ready to use them. When I open a jar, I place the peanut butter in a bowl and thoroughly mix the oil into the peanuts. Then I put it back in the jar and refrigerate it. It will not separate again as long as it is refrigerated. I know this sounds like a lot of trouble, but it's worth it for both the flavor and the nutritive value of fresh, additive-free peanut butter.
Sesame seeds. These are available two ways: Hulled sesame seeds are white and have a milder flavor than the un-hulled, brown kind. Both are fine for cooking.
Tahini. This is a sesame seed paste or butter that is made from ground, unhulled sesame seeds, and is a common ingredient in many traditional Middle Eastern dishes. It can be purchased in some grocery stores and in most health food stores. There is a recipe in this book to make your own tahini if you prefer. Tahini will separate, so be sure to mix in the oils before each use. Refrigerate after opening.
Sunflower seeds. Buy these raw or dry-roasted.
Walnuts

LEGUMES

Most legumes are available dried or canned. Use either kind in the recipes in this book. Canned beans are more convenient, but they're more expensive, and may contain extra salt. They can be rinsed to lower the salt content.
Garbanzos (chick-peas)
Lentils
Pinto beans
Red beans
Kidney beans
Tofu. Tofu is made from soy milk. It is a high-protein staple and can be used to replace dairy products. Tofu is sold in health food and Oriental food stores, or in the fresh-produce section of most grocery stores. It comes in either a soft or a firm version. For recipes calling for mashed tofu, the soft kind works best. For tofu cubes, such as those used in stir-fry recipes, the firm version is better. Keep tofu in the refrigerator just as you would cottage cheese. Be sure to read the dates on the package when purchasing. Most tofu will last only a week or so in the refrigerator. The water it comes in should be changed every few days.

There is a new brand of tofu available called Mori-Nu. It comes in "silken-firm" and "silken-soft" versions. It has a smoother consistency and a longer shelf life than ordinary tofu. It comes in a cardboard carton that, according to the manufacturer, locks out light, oxygen, and microorganisms that lead to early spoilage. If tofu has an odor, it is usually spoiled. Be sure to note expiration dates before using.

Tofu-powdered milk. This is my preference as a replacement for dairy milk or soy milk. It has a smoother texture and better flavor than soy milk. The brands that I have used and liked are Tofu White, by Magic Mill, and Better Than Milk. These are available at health food stores. Use this milk when you wish to replace dairy milk in recipes, over cereal, and for drinking.

FRUITS

DRIED FRUITS
Apricots
Coconut. The unsweetened type is better, and is usually available only in health food stores.
Currants. These are a nice change from raisins.
Dates, seedless
Raisins

CANNED FRUITS AND JUICES
Choose fruits that are juice packed or have no added sugar. Choose fruit juices that have no added sugar and contain no additives.
Coco Lopez. This is the brand name for a pastelike coconut mixture that is often used for making mixed drinks. You can usually find it with other drink mixers in the grocery store.
Cranberry juice
Lemon juice
Peaches

Pears
Pineapple chunks
Pinapple coconut juice. This is a very nice product, but unfortunately, it is available at only a few grocery stores. Search for it. It's worth the effort. It combines beautifully with all sorts of other juices to make wonderful punches and works great for flavoring sorbets.

FROZEN FRUITS
Be sure to buy juices that have no added sugar. When buying frozen fruits, get those that are individually quick frozen, with no added sugar.
Apple juice concentrate. This concentrate is naturally very sweet, and can be used to flavor and sweeten many dessert recipes.
Blueberries, whole
Lemon juice concentrate
Orange juice concentrate
Pineapple juice concentrate
Raspberries, whole
Strawberries, whole or sliced

VEGETABLES

FRESH VEGETABLES
Most fresh vegetables, of course, should be purchased as close to serving time as possible, so that you eat them at their peak of nutritive value and flavor. There are a few fresh vegetables, however, that keep well and can be bought ahead. These will last up to a month if refrigerated.
Carrots
Garlic cloves
Jicama. This versatile vegetable is also called the Mexican potato (and occasionally the Chinese yam). It grows in Mexico and other Central American countries, where it is eaten much like the white or Irish potato in the United States. Jicama is a brown tuber, resembling a turnip in appearance and a water chestnut in flavor

and consistency. In fact, its watery-crisp texture and bland taste are so similar to the water chestnut that it makes an excellent substitute for this more expensive vegetable. When purchasing jicama, look for firm, smooth, clean, well-shaped tubers that are free from cuts and bruises. Small tubers are best because large ones tend to be woody. The interior of a good jicama is white, crisp, and juicy. Peel and use jicamas raw or cook and serve as a potato. Store fresh jicamas in a plastic bag in the refrigerator. They will keep well for one to two weeks.

Onions, white or yellow

Potatoes. I like Russet potatoes for baking, and red potatoes for boiled or steamed potatoes. Keep a supply of nice white cooking potatoes on hand for use in recipes that call for grated or chopped potatoes that will be combined with other foods.

FROZEN VEGETABLES
Broccoli
Cauliflower
Carrots, sliced, and baby whole
Corn
Green beans
Peas
Spinach, chopped

CANNED VEGETABLES
Artichoke hearts. Canned artichoke hearts are available marinated or unmarinated. Unmarinated hearts are the lowest in salt and fat.
Catsup
Green chilies, chopped
Olives, black
Pimientos
Tomatoes, canned whole with low salt
Tomato paste, low salt

DAIRY PRODUCTS

Read labels carefully. Buy low-fat milk, cheeses, and sour creams. Skim milk and part skim cheeses have the very lowest fat content. Remember that even 2 percent milk is really 32 percent fat and that 1 percent milk is really 16 percent fat. Only skim milk is fat-free. The nutrition information in this book is based on your using skim milk and the part skim cheeses in the recipes.

Evaporated skim milk. This excellent product is one of the most-used dairy products in the book. Although it comes in a can, it should not be confused with canned sweetened condensed milk—a totally different and much less healthy product. And don't confuse it with powdered skim milk. Canned evaporated skim milk is a good replacement for cream or half-and-half in recipes. You can even use it to make an acceptable substitute for whipped cream. Just refrigerate it until it is very cold, then add a little sweetener and vanilla and whip it at high speed with an electric mixer for about six minutes. You'll never miss the extra fat.

Mozzarella cheese, part skim. This is a good low-fat cheese. It can be bought ahead, grated, and frozen for future use.

SEASONINGS AND HERBS

I prefer to use fresh herbs whenever possible for their wonderful flavor. Dried herbs should be stored in the refrigerator or freezer and used within a few months of purchasing. Just before adding either dried or fresh herbs to a recipe, crush them in your hands to release their flavor.

Basil leaves

Brewer's yeast flakes. This is edible brewer's yeast (*Saccharomyces Cerevisiae*) in flake form. Don't confuse it with the brown, powdered brewer's yeast product, which is very bitter. Good brewer's yeast flakes are yellow and have a cheeselike flavor. I use them for seasoning popcorn and wherever a cheese flavor is wanted. I use the brand name Kal.

Celery seed, ground
Celery leaves, crushed
Chives
Chili powder
Cinnamon, ground and sticks
Coconut extract
Coriander
Cumin
Dillweed, chopped
Garlic powder
G. Washington Broth. This powdered broth mix is available in Beefy Brown, Golden, or Onion flavoring. It has a vegetable oil base with no animal fat added, and is available at health food stores and some grocery stores.
Lemon peel, grated
McKay's Chicken-Style Seasoning. This is an excellent chicken-flavored seasoning for broth and soups. It has a vegetable oil base with no animal fat added. It is available at health food stores. You can also make your own chicken seasoning mix, using the recipe in the variation section of this book.
Mustard, dried
Onion powder
Onions, instant, toasted
Oregano leaves, chopped. There are two types of oregano, Italian and Mexican. They are very different in taste. Use Italian with Italian foods, and Mexican with Mexican foods.
Paprika. I prefer Hungarian paprika for its nice red color.
Parsley, chopped
Poppy seeds
Rosemary
Sage
Salt
Savory
Soy sauce, low salt
Thyme
Vanilla, white and regular. White va-nilla is nice when flavoring white or light-colored foods, such as ice cream or whipped toppings. It is usually available in grocery stores. The flavor is the same as regular vanilla. Be sure to use pure vanilla, not imitation. The flavor of pure vanilla cannot be imitated.

MISCELLANEOUS

Active dry yeast. Dry yeast comes in two types—regular and instant. If you use instant, let the dough rise only once. For instance, you can make the dough for bread and put it straight in the bread tins for the first and only rising. Be sure to read the label carefully to know which yeast you are buying. Use the yeast by the date listed on the package for the best results.
Baco Bits. This is a brand name for imitation bacon in bit-sized pieces, available at all grocery stores.
Brown sugar
Cornstarch. This is used for thickening sauces, soups, and gravies.
Carob chips. Carob is the ground dried fruit of the carob tree, which grows mostly in the Mediterranean region and the Middle East. Because products made from carob resemble chocolate, some people consider the fruit a chocolate substitute. Carob does not taste as rich as chocolate, but it has its own unique and pleasant flavor. It is low in fat, low in calories, and contains no caffeine. It is naturally sweet and contains fiber, calcium, phosphorus, and potassium.
  Carob is available in several forms: as powder or carob chips, in blocks for baking or cooking, and in powdered mixes for hot carob beverages. Carob chips are available at some grocery stores and all health food stores.
Club soda. A low-calorie carbonated

15

beverage that makes a nice addition to punches.

Honey, raw. Honey is used as the primary sweetener in this book. It is sugar in its fructose state, a form that is easier and quicker to digest than refined sugars. Processed honey is not as easily digested as raw honey. Check the labels when buying honey. Raw honey may be available only in your health food store. Note: There have been warnings about giving infants (under one year old) raw honey, due to a few cases of food poisoning in infants.

Molasses. Store molasses at room temperature before opening; then keep it in the refrigerator, where it will keep for up to three months.

Nonstick vegetable cooking spray. Pam is the most commonly known brand of this product, used for greasing pans or preparing a skillet for sauté-ing. It is a good way to save on fat without sacrificing flavor.

Tapioca. Instant brands work best for convenience

Vegetable oils. There are many oils to choose from. Be sure to read the tips about choosing oils in the Nutritional Goals section of this book. Keep oil in the refrigerator. Oil kept on the pantry shelf can turn rancid and lose its fresh flavor. It's important to store all your staples carefully to preserve their flavor. Food at the peak of its flavor requires less salt.

Canola oil. This is a mild-tasting vegetable oil, very low in polyunsaturated fats and high in monounsaturated fat.

Safflower oil or other vegetable oil.

Olive oil, cold pressed. Delicious in salads and other dishes where its distinctive flavor enhances the other ingredients, the oil is also high in monounsaturated fat.

▶ **Spring Morning Brunch**
▶ Patio Brunch
▶ Bridal Shower Brunch

◀ *A table for two, set in a sunny window, provides a green bower for a spring morning brunch. Ferns, wicker, and flowered chintz complete the scene.*

WHETHER it's a cozy, romantic, quiet time for two, or breakfast for a crowd—a beautiful spring day is all the excuse you need to make an occasion out of a weekend morning meal. And by planning ahead just a little, the cook can relax and enjoy the casual, leisurely weekend feeling, right along with the guests.

Bake the English Muffin Bread a day or two ahead of time and wrap it airtight to keep it fresh. Or bake it as far ahead as you like and freeze it. Both the Muesli Cereal and Potato Chive Squares may be made the day before and refrigerated.

When you come to the kitchen in the morning, yawn and stretch, and make the omelet fillings. Set the table in a sunny corner with a view of the outdoors. Just before serving time, whip up the omelets, and breakfast is ready. Now relax and enjoy yourself.

MUESLI CEREAL
Serves 6

1½ **cups rolled oats**
½ **large unpeeled apple, shredded and diced**
¼ **cup raisins**
¼ **cup unsweetened grated coconut, raw or toasted**
¼ **cup slivered or chopped almonds, raw or toasted**
1½ **cups canned crushed pineapple with juice or canned peaches with juice**
¼ **teaspoon salt**
1 **teaspoon vanilla**
1 **cup liquid—fruit juice, cashew nut milk (recipe in Variations section), tofu milk (found in health food stores), or water**

1. Combine first 6 ingredients in bowl.
2. Dissolve salt and vanilla in liquid of choice.
3. Pour over oat mixture and stir, mixing well.
4. Marinate 1 hour or overnight in refrigerator or cool place.
5. Serve as breakfast cereal with either fruit juice, cashew nut milk, tofu milk, or skim milk.
Variations: Just before serving, add one cup of your favorite fruit (peaches, blueberries, etc.) and garnish with slivered almonds, optional.

Makes about 4 cups.

POTATO CHIVE SQUARES
Serves 5-6

3 **potatoes, boiled and cooled**
¼ **cup chives, chopped**
2 **egg whites, beaten, or ½ cup tofu, blended smooth**
2 **tablespoons flour**
¼ **teaspoon garlic powder**
Salt to taste

1. Peel and grate the boiled potatoes.
2. Combine all ingredients. Mix well.

3. Pour into well-greased 9″ x 9″ baking dish.
4. Bake at 350° F for 45 minutes.
5. Cut into squares.
Variations: Mix in ⅛-¼ cup chopped chilies, or chopped green peppers, or chopped pimientos. Or add ½ cup grated cheese.

GARDEN PATCH YOLKLESS OMELET
Serves 1

4 **egg whites**
1 **tablespoon cold water**
1 **teaspoon margarine**
2 **tablespoons chopped green onions**
3 **to 4 fresh mushrooms, chopped**
¼ **to ½ cup cooked, chopped spinach**
1 **small garlic clove, minced, or garlic powder to taste**
¼ **cup of grated low-fat mozzarella cheese**
Salt to taste, optional
Fresh tomatoes, sliced

1. Sauté green onions, mushrooms, spinach, and minced garlic in small amount of water or margarine until tender.
2. Beat egg whites with 1 tablespoon of cold water.
3. In an 8-inch nonstick fry pan, melt the margarine over medium heat, and pour in the egg mixture. Cook omelet uncovered, tilting the pan occasionally so uncooked eggs will flow to the bottom.
4. While the top still looks moist and creamy add sautéed vegetables down the center of the omelet. Top with mozzarella cheese and add salt to taste if desired. Fold edges toward the center, reduce heat to low, cover, and allow to cook for 1 minute.
5. Slip omelet onto a warm plate and place in a 200° F oven to keep warm while remaining servings are being prepared.
6. Just before serving, garnish each omelet with tomato slices.

TOFU VEGETABLE SCRAMBLE

Serves 4

- 2 **cups firm tofu**
- ⅓ **cup chopped green onions, tops included**
- ⅓ **cup thinly sliced fresh mushrooms**
- ⅓ **cup chopped red or green peppers**
- 1½ **to 2 teaspoons basil, dried or fresh**
- ½ **teaspoon garlic powder or to taste**
- 1 **teaspoon margarine**
  Salt to taste, optional
- 4 **cherry tomatoes, thinly sliced, to garnish**
  Fresh parsley

1. In a nonstick skillet melt margarine. Add onions, mushrooms, peppers, basil, garlic powder, and salt if desired. Sauté on medium-high heat until tender.
2. Place tofu in a medium-sized bowl and mash with a fork. Add mashed tofu to skillet with vegetables.
3. Continue to sauté until tofu is lightly browned.
4. Place scrambled tofu on plate and garnish with sliced cherry tomatoes and fresh parsley.

ENGLISH MUFFIN BREAD

12-15 Slices

- 2½ **to 3 cups whole-wheat flour**
- 4½ **teaspoons whole-wheat gluten flour**
- 1 **package active dry yeast**
- 1 **tablespoon honey**
- ¾ **teaspoon salt**
  Cornmeal

1. In large mixer bowl, combine 1 cup of the whole-wheat flour, the whole-wheat gluten flour, and yeast.
2. Combine 1¼ cups warm water (115-120° F), honey, and salt and stir together. Add to dry mixture in bowl.
3. Hand Mixer Option: Beat at low speed with electric mixer for ½ minute, scraping bowl. Beat 3 minutes at high speed. By hand stir in enough remaining flour to make a soft dough. Shape into ball.

Bread Maker Option: Beat at low speed for ½ minute, scraping bowl. Beat 3 minutes at high speed. Mix in enough remaining flour to make a soft dough. Shape into ball.

4. Place in lightly oiled bowl; turn once to oil surface. Cover; let rise in warm place until doubled in size (about 1 hour). Punch down. Cover with towel; let rest 10 minutes. Oil a 1-quart ovenproof casserole; sprinkle with cornmeal. Place dough in the casserole; sprinkle top with cornmeal. Cover; let rise in warm place until doubled in size (30-45 minutes). Bake at 400° F for 40-45 minutes. Cover loosely with foil during last part of baking if top browns too quickly. Remove from casserole dish; cool on rack.

Makes 1 round loaf.

NUTRITIONAL ANALYSIS FOR MENU:
Spring Morning Brunch
Analysis based on 1 serving of each recipe listed in menu (based on your choice of one serving of either omelet or the Tofu Scramble). For individual recipe analysis, see Appendix.

	Nondairy Option	Dairy Option
Calories	588 kcal.	653 kcal.
Protein	32.85 g.; 75% USRDA	35.15 g.; 80% USRDA
Carbohydrate	83.42 g.	83.83 g.
Total Fat	18.70 g.	22.80 g.
Polyunsaturated Fat	8.446 g.	4.636 g.
Monounsaturated Fat	5.165 g.	10.09 g.
Saturated Fat	3.273 g.	6.263 g.
Cholesterol	0.000 mg.	16.20 mg.
Sodium	228.7 mg.; 10% USRDA	712.6 mg.; 32% USRDA
Iron	18.63 mg.; 103% USRDA	6.167 mg.; 34% USRDA
Calcium	374.8 mg.; 47% USRDA	391.8 mg.; 49% USRDA
Fiber	8.600 g.	9.878 g.

Nondairy Option
Diabetic Exchanges:
Milk: 0.0; Veg.: 1.6; Fruit: 2.2
Bread: 2.7; Meat: 3.1; Fat: 2.3

Dairy Option
Diabetic Exchanges:
Milk: 0.0; Veg.: 1.4; Fruit: 2.2
Bread: 2.7; Meat: 3.1; Fat: 3.812

BRUNCHES

► Spring Morning Brunch
► **Patio Brunch**
► Bridal Shower Brunch

*O*UR family loves to eat meals outside. The fresh air and sunshine stimulate everyone's appetites and contribute to the enjoyment of wholesome food. The children especially love the holiday atmosphere of eating outdoors. We often serve breakfast on the patio, because it combines the fun of a picnic with the convenience of being at home. And with a little planning ahead, the cook can relax and enjoy her family, too.

Here's a patio brunch menu you'll love because it's beautiful to look at, and delicious, and much of it can be prepared ahead of time. The children can help Daddy fire up the barbecue and do the final cooking of the food outside.

I like to make the waffles ahead of time and freeze them. The Potato Bacobit Balls can also be made ahead of time and frozen in sealed containers. You can prepare and assemble the mouthwatering Breakfast Kabobs the night before. Make the marinade ahead also and store it in a separate container until you're ready to cook the kabobs.

◄ *It's hard to imagine a more colorful way to start the day than with this delicious combination of nature's bounty.*

23

STRAWBERRY PECAN BELGIAN WAFFLES
(NONDAIRY)
Serves 5

- 1½ cups quick or regular rolled oats
- ½ cup whole-wheat flour
- 2½ to 3 cups water, soy milk, or tofu milk
- ⅓ cup pecans
- ¾ teaspoon salt
- 1 teaspoon vanilla
- 1½ tablespoons honey
- 1 tablespoon vegetable oil, optional

1. Blend all ingredients in blender on low or medium speed until smooth. Then blend at high speed for five seconds before pouring batter into iron. Batter will thicken as it sits, so add a few tablespoons of water and repeat high-speed blending before pouring each waffle. This will aerate batter and prevent heavy waffles.

2. Condition the waffle iron grids by spraying with Pam or brushing lightly with cooking oil while cold. If you use a nonstick waffle iron, you'll need to do this for the first waffle only. Condition grids after every 2-3 waffles if you use an ordinary waffle iron. These waffles will be lighter and the center of waffle will be more thoroughly cooked if you use a Belgian waffle iron, which has much larger and higher squares.

3. Pour approximately ⅔-¾ cup batter into a 6-inch Belgian waffle iron, pouring in as much batter as possible without spilling over.

4. Bake 6-8 minutes for a 4-inch waffle iron or 8-10 minutes for a 6-inch waffle iron. Larger irons may take 15-20 minutes. To prevent splitting the waffle, do not open lid for the first 6-8 minutes. Turn the waffle over when placing it on serving plate, because the bottom of the waffle has the nicer appearance.

5. To store: Cool leftover waffles on a wire rack, stack in plastic bags and freeze.

6. To reheat: For crisp waffles, reheat in the toaster, toaster oven, or on a cookie sheet in the oven for 5-10 minutes, or warm quickly under the broiler. For softer waffles, heat in a covered casserole for 10-15 minutes in a 350° F oven, or microwave, covered, on high for 1 minute.

Barbecue Option: Place frozen waffles on grill 4 inches from coals. Grill 3-4 minutes on each side or until crisp.

7. Serve with strawberries and top with nondairy whipped topping or Tofu Whipped Cream (see Variations section for recipe).

Makes 5 6-inch waffles.

STRAWBERRY PECAN OAT BRAN WAFFLES
Serves 8

- 1½ cups skim milk
- 3 tablespoons honey
- 3 tablespoons melted and cooled margarine
- ⅓ cup pecan pieces
- ⅔ cup whole wheat flour
- ⅔ cup all-purpose flour
- ¾ cup unprocessed oat bran
- ½ teaspoon salt
- 4 egg whites

1. Place milk, melted margarine, and honey in blender or large mixing bowl.

2. Combine flours, bran, and salt in separate bowl. Gradually add flour mixture to milk mixture, blending until smooth. Transfer batter to large mixing bowl. Stir in pecan pieces.

3. In separate bowl, beat reserved egg whites just until stiff, moist peaks form. Fold gently into batter.

4. Bake in preheated regular or Belgian waffle iron 3-4 minutes or until browned.

5. To store: Place cooled waffles in plastic bags and freeze.

6. To reheat: For crisp waffles, reheat in toaster, toaster oven, or on cookie sheet for 5-10 minutes in 350° F oven, or under the broiler.

For soft waffles: Heat in covered casserole for 10-15 minutes in 350-degree oven, or microwave, covered, on high for 1 minute.

Barbecue Option: Place frozen waffles on grill 4 inches from coals. Grill 3-4 minutes on each side or until crisp.

7. Serve with strawberries and top with nondairy whipped topping or Tofu Whipped Cream (see Variations section for recipe).

Makes 8 6-inch waffles.

BREAKFAST KABOBS
Serves 8

16 Potato Bacobit Balls (recipe following)
1 8¾-ounce can sugar-free peach slices, drained, reserving liquid
1 8-ounce can sugar-free pineapple chunks, drained, reserving liquid
¾ teaspoon vanilla
1 large green pepper, cut into ¾-inch strips
1 large red pepper, cut into ¾-inch strips
1 large onion, cut into wedges

1. Make up Potato Bacobit Ball recipe.
2. To prepare marinade sauce: In small bowl combine peach juice, pineapple juice, and vanilla. Set aside.
3. Barbecue Method: On wooden kabob sticks, alternate the peppers, onions, Potato Bacobit Balls, peaches, and pineapple. Arrange on barbecue grill 3 inches from hot coals for 20 minutes, turning frequently and brushing often with marinade sauce.
   Oven Method: Arrange on broiler pan and brush with marinade. Bake at 400° F for 20 minutes, turning and brushing with marinade 2-3 times during baking.

POTATO BACOBIT BALLS
Serves 8

1 large raw potato, finely grated
1 green onion, including green tops, sliced
1 tablespoon water
¼ cup Bacobits
1 slice bread, crumbled
¼ teaspoon sage
2 tablespoons low-fat milk or soy milk

1 egg or 2 egg whites, slightly beaten, or ¼ cup tofu mashed

1. Preheat oven to 400° F. Mix grated potatoes and chopped onions with water and microwave on high for 5-8 minutes or until potatoes are soft.
2. Add Bacobits, bread crumbs, sage, milk, and egg or tofu. Mix together thoroughly and refrigerate for 1-2 hours to thicken.
3. Shape into 16 ½- to ¾-inch balls. Bake on lightly greased cookie sheet for approximately 10 minutes or until lightly browned.

ORANGE JUBILEE
Serves 4

⅛ cup honey
8 ounces frozen orange juice concentrate
1 cup skim milk or soy milk
1 cup water
1 teaspoon vanilla
12 ice cubes
orange peel spirals to garnish

1. Place all ingredients in blender and blend at high speed about 30 seconds or until ice cubes are crushed.
2. Pour into serving glasses and garnish with orange peel spirals.

NUTRITIONAL ANALYSIS FOR MENU:
Patio Brunch
Analysis based on 1 serving of each recipe listed in menu. For individual recipe analysis, see Appendix.

	Nondairy Option	Dairy Option
Calories	455 kcal.	431.6 kcal.
Protein	13.99 g.; 32% USRDA	13.15 g.; 30% USRDA
Carbohydrate	77.6 g.	73.33 g.
Fat	12.47 g.	11.62 g.
Polyunsaturated Fat	4.682 g.	2.332 g.
Monounsaturated Fat	4.267 g.	4.687 g.
Total Saturated Fat	1.357 g.	2.337 g.
Cholesterol	0.000 mg.	0.750 mg.
Sodium	361.6 mg.; 16% USRDA	301.6 mg.; 14% USRDA
Iron	5.195 mg.; 29% USRDA	4.555 mg.; 25% USRDA
Calcium	109.9 mg.; 14% USRDA	141.1 mg.; 18% USRDA
Fiber	7.171 g.	5.721 g.

Nondairy Option
Diabetic Exchanges:
Milk: 0.2; Veg.: 0.7; Fruit: 2.5
Bread: 2.0; Meat: 0.4; Fat: 2.5

Dairy Option
Diabetic Exchanges:
Milk: 0.3; Veg.: 0.6; Fruit: 2.5
Bread: 1.5; Meat: 0.3; Fat: 2.57

BRUNCHES

▶Spring Morning Brunch
▶Patio Brunch
▶**Bridal Shower Brunch**

*I*T'S *a beautiful weekend morning. Eliza's getting married next Sunday; and her closest friends are honoring her today with a bridal shower brunch. And "here comes the bride" doesn't have to mean "here come the calories and the cholesterol." So set a buffet table on the patio, get out the candles and your nicest china, and don't forget Eliza's favorite red roses.*

The cook won't miss a single rustle of tissue paper or one bit of friendly gossip, because this menu can be prepared almost entirely in advance. Make the Spinach Cheese Puffs and tomato sauce the day before and place in sealed containers for refrigeration overnight, or make them several days ahead and freeze them. Prepare and assemble the Potato Onion Blintzes and refrigerate, or if you prefer, lay crepes flat with wax paper in between each crepe to freeze. Then assemble blintzes just before serving. Make and freeze the Summer Fruit Ice-Cream Pie, the Cinnamon Nut Braid, and the Apricot Twist as far ahead as you wish.

◀ *The garden of a Mediterranean-style villa, built in 1908, provides this spectacular setting. The shrubbery and paths are laid out in the shape of the shadow the house casts just before sunset —a romantic notion if there ever was one.*

SPINACH CHEESE PUFFS
Serves 6-8

2 egg whites
1 cup (8 ounces) ricotta cheese
½ cup fine, dry bread crumbs
½ cup finely grated mozzarella cheese
¼ teaspoon garlic powder
½ teaspoon onion powder
½ teaspoon dry basil
½ teaspoon dry oregano
½ teaspoon thyme
1 package (10 ounces) frozen chopped spinach, thawed
All-purpose flour
Salt to taste, optional
Fresh Tomato Sauce (recipe following)

1. In a large bowl, beat egg whites until frothy. Add ricotta and mix well.
2. Stir in bread crumbs, grated mozzarella cheese, garlic powder, onion powder, salt to taste if desired. Blend in basil, oregano, and thyme.
3. Squeeze spinach gently with hands to remove excess moisture. Stir spinach into ricotta mixture.
4. Shape mixture into 1½-inch balls. Roll in flour to coat lightly.
5. Arrange puffs on lightly oiled or Pam-sprayed cookie sheet and cover with foil. Bake at 400° F for 20 minutes, turning puffs once during cooking. Uncover and bake 5 more minutes to brown.
6. Place puffs in a serving dish and pour Fresh Tomato Sauce over them.

TOFU SPINACH CHEESE PUFFS
Serves 8-10

1 10-ounce package frozen chopped spinach
1 cup tofu
6 tablespoons gluten flour
⅛ teaspoon ground rosemary
⅛ teaspoon thyme
1 teaspoon McKay's Chicken-style Seasoning, or chickenlike substitute (see Variations section)
½ cup bread crumbs
¼ teaspoon garlic powder
½ teaspoon onion powder
1 teaspoon salt, or to taste, optional
Fresh Tomato Sauce (recipe following)

1. Thaw spinach completely. Strain thoroughly and reserve water in case more moisture is needed in the mix.
2. Combine bread crumbs, garlic powder, onion powder, and gluten flour; mix well. Add spinach and finely mashed tofu and mix with hands if needed. Add salt to taste if desired. Form into ½-inch balls. If mixture is too dry, add a bit of the spinach juice.
3. Arrange balls on nonstick, lightly oiled or Pam-sprayed cookie sheet, cover with aluminum foil, and bake for 20 minutes at 400° F. May be uncovered and baked a bit longer to brown. May be frozen before or after baking. Just before serving, pour the Fresh Tomato Sauce over the balls and warm through.

Makes 18-20 1-inch balls.

FRESH TOMATO SAUCE
1½ tablespoons margarine or water
1 medium-sized onion, chopped
2 large tomatoes, peeled and finely chopped
1 cup water
½ teaspoon dry basil
¼ teaspoon salt to taste, optional
½ teaspoon oregano
½ teaspoon thyme

1. In a 2-quart pan over medium heat, sauté chopped onion in margarine or water until soft.
2. Add the tomatoes, water, basil, oregano, and thyme. Add salt to taste, if desired.
3. Bring to a boil over high heat and cook for 10 minutes, stirring frequently; then reduce heat to medium and continue cooking, stirring occasionally, until sauce has thickened.
4. Pour the tomato sauce over the Spinach Cheese Puffs and serve.

POTATO ONION BLINTZES

Serves 12-16

16 **French Crepes, (recipe following), or Cholesterol-free Crepes (recipe following)**
1 **teaspoon margarine or water**
1 **large onion, finely chopped**
2 **cups mashed, unseasoned cooked potatoes (3 medium-sized potatoes)**
1 **egg white or ¼ cup tofu blended smooth**
½ **teaspoon salt, or to taste, optional**
½ **teaspoon garlic powder**

Topping

1 **cup sour cream or plain yogurt or Nondairy Tofu Sour Cream topping (see Variations section)**
1 **cup finely chopped chives or green onions**
Salt to taste, if desired

1. In a small skillet over medium heat, sauté onion in margarine or water until golden brown. (If using water, cover pan during cooking and watch carefully to prevent sticking.)

2. Stir cooked onion into mashed potatoes.

3. Beat egg white or tofu and stir into potatoes. Add salt to taste, if desired. Add garlic powder.

4. For each blintz, place a crepe, browned side up, on a flat surface. Spoon about 2 tablespoons of the potato mixture onto center of crepe. Fold opposite sides over center so they overlap slightly, then fold the bottom toward the center and roll top down to enclose.

5. Place folded side down on a pan or tray. Repeat until all crepes are filled. If desired, you may store blintzes at this point, covered, in refrigerator until the next day.

6. Before serving, place blintzes folded side down on lightly oiled or Pam-sprayed cookie sheet, and bake at 400° F for 10-15 minutes or until lightly browned. Cover blintzes and keep warm in low-temperature oven until serving time.

7. Serve hot with sour cream, yogurt, or Nondairy Tofu Sour Cream and chives.

Makes 16 blintzes.

FRENCH CREPES

(Dairy Option)

1 **cup all-purpose flour or whole-wheat flour**
1¾ **cups skim milk**
¼ **cup cold water**
2 **eggs**
1 **tablespoon safflower oil or any vegetable oil**
¼ **teaspoon salt, optional**

1. Place all ingredients in a food processor or blender and process until smooth. Cover and refrigerate a minimum of 10 minutes or up to 2 hours.

2. Spray with Pam or lightly oil a 10-inch nonstick skillet; heat over medium high heat. Remove from heat and pour a scant ⅓ cup of batter into the middle of the pan. Quickly tilt the pan in a circular motion so that the batter evenly forms a crepe approximately 8-inches in diameter.

3. Return the pan to the heat for about 1 minute. When the edges of the crepe begin to pull away from the pan, flip the crepe over and lightly brown the other side for about ½ minute.

4. Remove crepe from pan to cool. Repeat this procedure with the remaining batter. (These crepes are delicious and light even when they're made with whole-wheat flour).

Makes about 16 8-inch crepes.

CHOLESTEROL-FREE OAT CREPES

(Nondairy Option)

- ¾ **cup whole-wheat flour**
- ¾ **cup quick, rolled oats**
- 2 **cups tofu milk, soy milk, Cashew-Rice Milk (see Variations section for recipe), or skim milk**
- 1 **tablespoon safflower oil or any vegetable oil**
- ½ **teaspoon salt**
- 1 **teaspoon honey**

1. Place all ingredients in a food processor or blender and process until smooth. Let stand 10 minutes.

2. Spray with Pam or lightly oil a 10-inch nonstick skillet or crepe pan; heat over medium-high heat. Remove pan from heat and pour a scant ⅓ cup batter into the middle of the pan. Quickly tilt the pan in a circular motion until the batter evenly forms an 8-inch crepe. If the batter gets too thick and does not spread easily, add water, one tablespoon at a time, whizzing in blender after each addition until mixture is thin and easy to spread in skillet.

3. Return the pan to the heat for about 1 minute or until bottom of crepe is lightly browned. Flip the crepe over and lightly brown the other side for about ½ minute.

4. Remove crepe from pan to cool. Repeat this procedure with the remaining batter. These crepes are very good; you'll never miss the eggs, and your body won't miss the cholesterol.

Makes 16 8-inch crepes.

SUMMER FRUIT ICE-CREAM PIE

Serves 8-10

- 2 **pints low-fat vanilla ice cream, slightly softened, or Piña Colada Tofu Ice Cream (recipe following)**
- 1 **Oatmeal-Wheat Germ Cookie Crust (recipe following)**
- 3 **cups mixed fruits (blueberries, raspberries, sliced strawberries, and peaches)**
- 1 **kiwi fruit, peeled and cut in small wedges**
- ½ **cup raspberry puree (recipe following)**
  Mint sprigs to garnish

1. Spread half the ice cream over crust; add half the fruits (except the kiwi).

2. Using a large serving spoon, spread remaining ice cream over top of fruit layer.

3. Freeze at least 3 hours or overnight.

4. Before serving, top with remaining fruits, including kiwi; drizzle with raspberry puree and garnish with mint sprigs.

5. Refrigerate about 10 minutes to soften ice cream slightly.

Makes 8-10 servings.

PIÑA COLADA TOFU ICE CREAM

- 1¼ **cups tofu**
- 5 **tablespoons oil**
- 3 **tablespoons honey**
- ¾ **teaspoon lemon juice**
- ⅛ **teaspoon salt**
- 2 **teaspoons vanilla (use white vanilla for a whiter color)**
- 1 **small banana**
- 1 **cup pineapple-coconut juice or 1 cup pineapple juice and ½ teaspoon cocunut extract**

1. Blend all ingredients until smooth and creamy.

2. Pour into ice-cube trays or 2-inch muffin pans. (Spray the muffin pans with Pam first for easier removal). Freeze solid.

3. Just before serving, remove from trays and place in food processor. Process just until smooth and creamy, approximately 2 minutes. Use to make Summer Fruit Ice-Cream Pie.

Makes approximately 4 cups.

RASPBERRY PUREE SAUCE

2 cups fresh or frozen raspberries
5 tablespoons honey, optional
1 teaspoon grated lemon peel, optional
2 teaspoons cornstarch, optional
¼ cup water, optional

1. Puree raspberries in blender or food processor. Strain pureed raspberries to remove seeds. You may use sauce at this stage. If you prefer a sweeter, thicker sauce, continue with steps 2 and 3.
2. In small saucepan, combine the raspberry puree, honey, and lemon peel. Stir over low heat until mixture almost comes to a boil.
3. In a small cup, dissolve the cornstarch in the water, mixing with a fork until smooth; add to raspberry mixture. Continue to cook mixture slowly until thick and smooth. Cover and chill.

Makes approximately 2 cups.

OATMEAL-WHEAT GERM COOKIE CRUST

¾ cup quick or rolled oats
½ cup wheat germ
4 tablespoons whole-wheat flour
¼ cup walnuts or pecans, finely chopped
½ teaspoon ground cinnamon, or Cinnamon Substitute (see Variations section)
⅓ cup honey
¼ cup margarine
1 teaspoon vanilla

1. Preheat oven to 375° F. Lightly oil a 9-inch pie plate.
2. Combine the rolled oats, wheat germ, flour, nuts, and cinnamon.
3. Melt the margarine with the honey; add the vanilla. Stir into the oats mixture, blending well.
4. Press with fingers into pie plate. Bake 8-12 minutes, or until lightly browned.

Makes 1 piecrust.

APRICOT TWIST

Serves 25-30

3¼ cups unsifted whole-wheat flour
4½ teaspoons whole-wheat gluten flour
1 teaspoon salt
1 package active dry yeast
⅔ cup warm water (115-120° F)
2 tablespoons melted margarine
¼ cup honey
2 eggs or 4 egg whites at room temperature, or ½ cup tofu, mixed with 3 tablespoons water and blended smooth
Apricot Filling (recipe following)
Crumb Topping (recipe following)

1. In large bowl, blend 1 cup of the whole-wheat flour, gluten flour, salt, and yeast.
2. Combine warm water (115-120° F), margarine, and honey.
3. Combine liquid mixture, tofu or eggs (be sure tofu or eggs are at room temperature), and dry ingredients. Beat for 2 minutes with electric mixer or 5 minutes by hand. Stir in remaining 2-2¼ cups whole-wheat flour, adding ½ cup at a time.
4. Turn out onto floured surface and knead until smooth and elastic (8-10 minutes). Place in oiled bowl, turn once to oil top, and let rise in warm place until doubled in size (about 1 hour).
5. Punch down dough and divide in half. Cover with towel and let stand while preparing filling. Then, with a lightly floured rolling pin, roll out each half of dough into an 8″ x 14″ rectangle.
6. Place each dough rectangle on an oiled cookie sheet. Slit dough at 1-inch intervals down each side, leaving an uncut middle area approximately 3 inches wide for filling. Spread half of Apricot Filling down the middle of each rectangle.
7. Lift and crisscross sides over top of filling, beginning at top and working toward the bottom, creating a twisted or braided effect.
8. Cover loosely with a towel and let rise in warm place until doubled in size. Brush each twist with melted margarine if desired, and sprinkle on Crumb Topping (recipe following).

9. Bake at 350° F for 20 minutes. Remove from cookie sheet and cool on wire rack.

Makes 2 long twist loaves.

APRICOT FILLING

1½ cups dried apricots, chopped
1 cup apple juice
½ cup honey or brown sugar

1. In a small saucepan, combine the apricots and apple juice and bring to a boil. Let simmer 20-25 minutes.
2. Remove from heat and stir in honey or brown sugar. Place half of mixture in center of each apricot twist.

CRUMB TOPPING

⅓ cup whole-wheat flour
2 tablespoons honey or brown sugar
1½ teaspoons cinnamon or Cinnamon Substitute (see Variations section)
2 tablespoons margarine, melted

1. Mix all ingredients until crumbly. Sprinkle half of mixture on top of each apricot twist.

CINNAMON NUT BRAID

Serves 15-18

3 cups whole-wheat flour
4½ teaspoons whole-wheat gluten flour
2 packages active dry yeast
½ cup warm water (115-120° F)
¼ cup margarine
¼ cup honey
½ teaspoon salt
1 egg, 2 egg whites, or ¼ cup tofu, blended smooth

Filling

4 to 6 tablespoons margarine
Cinnamon to taste, or Cinnamon Substitute (see Variations section)
½ cup nuts, chopped
4 to 6 tablespoons brown sugar or honey
½ cup raisins, optional

1. In large mixing bowl, combine 1 cup whole-wheat flour, 4½ teaspoons whole-wheat gluten flour, and 2 packages active dry yeast.
2. In saucepan heat ½ cup water, ¼ cup margarine, ¼ cup honey, and ½ teaspoon salt just until warm (115-120° F), stirring to melt margarine.
3. Add liquid mixture and eggs or tofu (be sure eggs or tofu are at room temperature) to dry flour-yeast mixture in bowl. Beat at low speed with electric mixer for ½ minute, scraping sides of bowl constantly. Beat 3 minutes at high speed. By hand, stir in remaining 2 cups flour to make a moderately soft dough.
4. Turn out on lightly floured surface and knead till smooth and elastic (8-10 minutes). Shape into a ball. Place in lightly oiled bowl, turning once to oil top of dough. Cover with a towel and let rise in warm place until doubled in size (about 1 hour).
5. Punch dough down; turn out on lightly floured surface. Divide in thirds. Cover with towel; let rest for 10 minutes. With lightly floured rolling pin, roll each portion into a 16″ x 4″ rectangle.
6. Spread each rectangle with margarine, sprinkle with cinnamon, nuts, and raisins, if desired. Sprinkle brown sugar or drizzle honey on each rectangle.
7. Roll up each rectangle from long side to make rope. Pinch seam to seal. Line up the three ropes, 1 inch apart, on oiled baking sheet. Pinch top ends together and tuck under. Braid the three ropes together loosely to the bottom. Pinch bottom ends together and tuck under.
8. Cover with towel and let rise in warm place till doubled in size (about 45 minutes). Bake at 375° F for 25 minutes. Cover loosely with foil for the last 15 minutes to prevent overbrowning.

Makes 1 braid.

NUTRITIONAL ANALYSIS FOR MENU:
Bridal Shower Brunch

Analysis based on 1 serving of each recipe listed in menu, except the sweet breads and cheese puffs. Menu analysis was based on 1 serving of only one bread listed, and one serving of one cheese puff. For individual recipe analysis, see Appendix.

	Nondairy Option	Dairy Option
Calories	769 kcal.	623 kcal.
Protein	28.22 g.; 64% USRDA	24.99 g. 57% USRDA
Carbohydrate	107.6 g.	89.60 g.
Total Fat	30.16 g.	22.07 g.
Polyunsaturated Fat	14.68 g.	8.811 g.
Monounsaturated Fat	8.382 g.	6.251 g.
Saturated Fat	4.160 g.	4.994 g.
Cholesterol	0.000 mg.	49.10 mg.
Sodium	400.1 mg.; 18% USRDA	346.4 mg.; 16% USRDA
Iron	15.82 mg.; 82% USRDA	8.268 mg.; 46% USRDA
Calcium	324.4 mg.; 41% USRDA	390.3 mg.; 49% USRDA
Fiber	10.97 g.	9.720 g.

Nondairy Option
Diabetic Exchanges:
Milk: 0.1; Veg.: 1.9; Fruit: 1.8
Bread: 3.1; Meat: 1.9; Fat: 4.9

Dairy Option
Diabetic Exchanges:
Milk: 0.2; Veg.: 1.3; Fruit: 1.5
Bread: 2.4; Meat: 1.9; Fat: 3.4

►Greek Luncheon
►The Better Burger and Fries
►Luncheon on the Med
►Finnish Summer Delight

*T*HE ancient Greeks were hardy indi-
vidualists. They believed in the perfection
of mind and body. The Greek climate is
dry and exhilarating, and gifted with the
most magical combination of brilliant
sunlight and deep blue sky. It encourages
a healthy, outdoor life.

This menu reflects both the Greek
spirit and the Greek climate. It is simple,
healthy, and delicious. And like a classi-
cal Greek sculpture, it is also a feast for
the eye. Choose a sunny day to try this
delightful luncheon in an outdoor setting.

You can make the Gyro Sandwiches
quickly and easily if you have pita bread
on hand. Since it freezes beautifully (and
gets eaten so fast), you'd be wise to prepare a large quantity at a time and keep
it in the freezer. Then you'll be ready for
those last-minute drop-in guests. (Of
course, you can also purchase ready-
made pita bread, but nothing can com-
pare with the just-baked flavor of homemade.)

◄ *Serve this menu outdoors if possible.*
Choose serving dishes with simple designs
and strong colors, like this Fiesta Ware. An
antique wooden cutlery box makes a unique
server for the Gyro Sandwiches.

VEGETARIAN GYRO SANDWICH

Serves 1

> 1 **pita bread (see recipe following)**
> ½ to ¾ **cup lettuce, chopped**
> ¼ **cup chopped tomatoes**
> 1 **teaspoon sliced green onions with tops**
> 1 **tablespoon crumbled feta cheese or Nondairy Pimento Cheese (recipe in Variations section)**
> 1 to 2 **tablespoons Cucumber Yogurt Dressing (see recipe following) Black olives, sliced, to garnish, optional**

1. Prepare Homemade Pita Bread (recipe following).

2. Open pocket and fill with lettuce, tomatoes, green onions, and cheese. Top with dressing and garnish with black olives, if desired. Serve. Note: Nutrition analysis for menu is based on 2 gyro sandwiches per serving.

HOMEMADE PITA BREAD

> 1 **cup water**
> 1 **cup apple juice**
> 1½ **tablespoons active dry yeast**
> ½ **tablespoon salt**
> 4 to 5 **cups whole-wheat flour**
> 6 **teaspoons whole-wheat gluten flour, optional**
> **Yellow cornmeal**

1. In saucepan, combine water and apple juice and heat just until warm (about 115° F). Put warm liquid in large mixing bowl, sprinkle yeast over liquid and allow to dissolve. Add 2 cups flour and the 6 teaspoons whole-wheat gluten flour, if desired; beat at medium speed of electric mixer for 3 minutes. Cover and let rise in warm place until doubled in size, about 15-20 minutes.

2. Add salt. Beat in as much flour as can be beaten vigorously by hand for 6 minutes. Mix as much remaining flour as can be handled when mixing by hand and enough so that dough can be removed from bowl onto a floured surface. Cover with a towel and let rest for 10 minutes.

3. Knead gently and rhythmically for 10-15 minutes. Keeping dough rolled in a ball, add the remaining flour, a little at a time, kneading after each addition. Be careful not to add too much flour, or the bread will be dry. Keep dough slightly sticky to the touch. Cover with a towel and let rest 10 minutes.

4. At this point, the dough may be shaped into pita bread, loaves of bread, pizza dough, buns, etc. To make pitas, cut dough in half. With lightly floured hands, roll each half into a rope 2½ inches in diameter. Cut each roll into pieces, and roll with hands into 2- to 3-inch balls, depending on the desired size of pocket bread.

5. Place each dough ball on flat surface and, with a lightly floured rolling pin, roll out from center until dough forms a circle ¼-inch thick. Gently dip bottom of dough in cornmeal and place on back of cookie sheet. Cover with a towel and let rise at room temperature for 15 minutes.

6. The best way to bake pitas is on flat quarry tiles, which can be purchased at any rock and stone outlet. A cast-iron skillet turned upside down also works well, but limits you to making one pita at a time. A third option, less satisfactory than the others but still workable, is a cookie sheet turned upside down.

7. Place one of the three items mentioned above in the oven and preheat to 500° F. Remove top oven rack for convenience in removing pitas later.

8. Gently but quickly slip a raised pita onto a spatula and place it on the hot tile, skillet, or cookie sheet. Once it touches the hot surface, you cannot move it, so aim carefully. Repeat with as many pitas as your baking method will accommodate. Close oven and bake for 3-4 minutes or until lightly browned. (If you're baking the pitas on a cookie sheet, you may see very few or perhaps no bubbles appear—do not overcook just because bubbles are small and not uniform. If you're using tiles or a cast-iron skillet, you will be able to watch pockets form immediately).

9. Remove pitas carefully from oven with spatula and place on cooling rack. Cut each pita in half while it is still warm. If difficult to

cut, place pita in a damp towel for 5 minutes, and then it will cut nicely.

10. To store: Place in plastic bags, 3 or 4 to a bag, while still slightly warm to keep soft. May be frozen.

Makes approximately 25-30.

GREEK SALAD WITH LEMON-GARLIC DRESSING
Serves 6-8

½ **head iceberg lettuce, torn into bite-size pieces**
1 **bunch romaine lettuce or green leaf lettuce, torn into bite-size pieces**
1 **cucumber, thinly sliced**
3 **green onions with tops, thinly sliced**
6 **to 8 radishes, sliced**
3 **tomatoes, cut into eight wedges each**
12 **to 18 Greek or black olives, optional**
Feta cheese, crumbled, to garnish, optional
Lemon-Garlic Dressing (see Variations section)

1. Arrange greens in center of large platter. (For the most authentic and delicious Greek salad, choose a wooden platter and rub it with garlic before arranging greens.)
2. Cover greens with row of sliced cucumbers.
3. Sprinkle cucumbers with sliced green onions.
4. Surround cucumbers with sliced radishes.
5. Encircle edge of platter with tomato wedges.
6. Garnish with olives and sprinkle with feta cheese if desired. Serve with Lemon-Garlic Dressing (recipe in Variations section).
Note: Nutrition analysis is based on ½ tablespoon of dressing per serving.

CHEESE AND GARLIC TOASTED PITA CHIPS
Serves 4-8

8 **pieces of pita bread**
2 **tablespooons margarine, optional**
2 **tablespoons Parmesan Cheese or Nondairy Parmesan Cheese (see Variations section), optional**
Garlic powder or garlic salt to taste

1. Cut pita bread halves into 3-4 pie-shaped wedges.
2. Melt margarine and brush lightly onto each wedge, inside and outside, if desired. If you choose not to use margarine, you may wish to lightly brush the pita pieces with water to help seasonings to stick to bread.
3. Sprinkle each wedge with parmesan cheese and garlic powder. Sprinkle with salt to taste if desired.
4. Bake in preheated 400° F oven for about 10 minutes, watching carefully to avoid burning. These may also be baked in a 250° F oven for 30 minutes or until very crispy.
Note: Nutrition analysis is based on 4 8-chip servings.

Makes 32 large pita chip wedges or 8 4-chip servings or 4 8-chip servings.

NUTRITIONAL ANALYSIS FOR MENU:
Greek Luncheon
Analysis based on 1 serving of each recipe listed in menu. For individual recipe analysis, see Appendix.

	Nondairy Option	Dairy Option
Calories	457 kcal.	435 kcal.
Protein	17.29 g.; 39% USRDA	18.01 g.; 41% USRDA
Carbohydrate	73.02 g.	67.62 g.
Total Fat	14.03 g.	12.93 g.
Polyunsaturated Fat	3.854 g.	0.904 g.
Monounsaturated Fat	5.972 g.	5.112 g.
Saturated Fat	2.028 g.	5.314 g.
Cholesterol	0.000 mg.	25.40 mg.
Sodium	640.3 mg.; 29% USRDA	790.3 mg.; 36% USRDA
Iron	7.595 mg.; 42% USRDA	5.055 mg.; 28% USRDA
Calcium	131.5 mg.; 16% USRDA	265.1 mg.; 33% USRDA
Fiber	14.90 g.	13.22 g.

Nondairy Option Diabetic Exchanges:	Dairy Option Diabetic Exchanges:
Milk: 0.0; Veg.: 2.4; Fruit: 0.3	Milk: 0.2; Veg.: 2.2; Fruit: 0.3
Bread: 3.5; Meat: 0.6; Fat: 2.2	Bread: 3.3; Meat: 0.6; Fat: 2.1

LUNCHEONS

▶ Greek Luncheon
▶ **The Better Burger and Fries**
▶ Luncheon on the Med
▶ Finnish Summer Delight

*Y*OU *deserve a break today" begins a popular hamburger chain's famous commercial. And the burger on a bun with fries is no doubt the modern family's favorite quick and easy lunch. Now you can give your family and friends a real break with this vegetarian, low-fat burger and fries menu.*

Make plenty of the delicious wholewheat buns and Garden Nut Burgers. Extras can be frozen for later use. Make the Fresh Vegetable Basil Soup and boil the potatoes a day ahead of time if you wish.

Just before serving, cut and bake the fries, warm the soup, and prepare the toppings for the sandwiches. Then sit down with the gang and watch them dig in.

◀ *If you want to teach your children to prefer healthful food, these tasty burgers and unfried "fries" are the perfect place to start.*

GARDEN NUT BURGERS
SERVES 16

Dairy option:

- 2 **eggs, beaten (or substitute 4 egg whites to lower cholesterol)**
- 1 **cup low-fat cottage cheese**
  Nondairy option: Replace eggs and cottage cheese with 1½ cups tofu, blended smooth
- 1 **cup bread crumbs**
- 1 **cup uncooked oats**
- 1 **medium onion, grated or finely chopped**
- ¼ to ½ **cup carrots, grated very fine**
- 1 **teaspoon garlic powder**
- 1 **teaspoon McKay's Chicken Seasoning, Chickenlike Seasoning (see Variations section), or any dehydrated chicken seasoning made with vegetable fat**
- 2 **tablespoons margarine, melted, optional**

1. Mix all above ingredients well.
2. Form with hands into medium-sized patties.
3. Lightly coat nonstick skillet with oil. Brown patties. Or place uncooked patties on lightly oiled nonstick cookie sheet and bake at 350° F for 20-30 minutes or until nicely browned. Turn once during cooking.
4. Serve in whole wheat buns (recipe following). May be used also as an entrée served with your favorite sauce or gravy. May be frozen for later use.

Makes about 16 patties.

HOMEMADE WHOLE WHEAT BUNS

- 1 **cup warm water (115-120° F)**
- 1 **tablespoon honey**
- 1 **package active dry yeast**
- 1 **teaspoon salt**
- 2 **tablespoons oil, optional**
- 2 to 2¼ **cups whole-wheat flour**
- 4 **teaspoons whole-wheat gluten flour**
- 6 **tablespoons wheat germ**

1. Dissolve honey in water, then stir in yeast. Let stand until yeast begins to bubble, 5-8 minutes.
2. Stir in salt. Add oil, if desired. Add 1 cup whole-wheat flour, whole-wheat gluten flour, and wheat germ. Beat vigorously about 1 minute. Add 1 cup more flour, mix well. Add only enough more flour so that dough does not stick to hands.
3. Knead dough on lightly floured work surface about 5 minutes, working in more flour if necessary. Place dough in large oiled bowl. Turn once to oil top of dough. Cover with a towel and let rise in a warm place until doubled in size, 30-45 minutes.
4. Punch down, knead briefly. Be sure to squeeze out all air bubbles.
5. Form into loaf or shape into buns. To make buns: Divide dough into 6-8 balls. Turn balls in hands folding edges to make even circles. Flatten balls on lightly floured surface to form into 3½- to 4-inch buns. Arrange buns on oiled baking sheets and let rise in warm place until doubled in size, about 30-40 minutes.
6. Bake in preheated 375° F oven for 12-15 minutes or until golden brown. Or bake loaf for 35 minutes. (Do not overbake; overbaking may cause hard buns). Cool on a rack.
7. To store: Cool and place in sealed container or plastic bags to keep soft. May also be frozen.
8. To reheat: Place rolls in a paper bag. Sprinkle or mist a small amount of water on outside of bag. Fold top down and microwave rolls in bag 1 minute on medium high or heat in oven for 5-10 minutes at 250° F.

Makes 6-8 sandwich buns.

FRESH VEGETABLE BASIL SOUP
Serves 10

- 1 **tablespoon margarine, optional**
- 1 **medium-sized onion, chopped**
- 1 **large stalk celery, sliced**
- 1 to 2 **carrots, sliced ⅛-inch thick**
- 1 **large or 2 medium-sized potatoes, peeled and cubed**
- 2 **large tomatoes, peeled and diced**

4 cups water
3 tablespoons coarsely chopped
   fresh basil, or 2 teaspoons dried
   basil
3 teaspoons garlic powder
1 bay leaf
1 teaspoon thyme
2 tablespoons dried parsley
½ small head cauliflower, broken into
   flowerets
2 small zucchini, sliced ¼-inch thick
½ pound fresh green peas, (shelled)
   or frozen (unthawed)
   Salt to taste, optional
   Parmesan cheese to garnish, optional, or Nondairy Parmesan
   Cheese (see Variations section)

1. In a 5-quart pan over medium heat, melt margarine, if desired. Add onion, celery, and carrots; cook, stirring occasionally, until vegetables are soft but not brown (about 10 minutes). (If deleting margarine, add small amount of water to pan and add vegetables, cover and let steam until tender and continue with regular recipe).

2. Meanwhile, peel potato and cut into ½-inch cubes. Peel and dice tomatoes to make at least 2 cups. Add to other ingredients in pan the potatoes, tomatoes, additional water, basil, garlic powder, bay leaf, thyme, and parsley. Bring to a boil, then cover and let simmer for 15 minutes.

3. Add cauliflower and zucchini and simmer for 10 more minutes. Add peas and simmer for another 5 minutes, or until all vegetables are tender. Season to taste with salt if desired.

4. Serve. Sprinkle individual servings with Parmesan cheese, if desired, or Nondairy Parmesan Cheese. Garnish with a small celery heart stalk with the leaves still attached, if desired.

Makes about 10 cups.

UNFRIED FRENCH FRIES
Serves 4-6

6 medium to large potatoes
Salt to taste, optional
Vegetable oil, optional

1. Boil potatoes 20 minutes. (Peel them or leave them unpeeled.)

2. Cut as fries. Place on lightly oiled cookie sheet, one layer thick. Lightly sprinkle with salt, if desired, or your favorite seasonings. Brush fries lightly with oil if desired, but this is not necessary.

3. Bake at 400° F for 45-60 minutes. Turn with a spatula after 25 minutes. Serve.

NUTRITIONAL ANALYSIS FOR MENU:
The Better Burger and Fries
Analysis based on 1 serving of each recipe listed in menu.
For individual recipe analysis, see Appendix.

	Nondairy Option	Dairy Option
Calories	479.3 kcal.	578 kcal.
Protein	20.33 g.; 46% USRDA	24.03 g.; 55% USRDA
Carbohydrate	89.00 g.	85.10 g.
Total Fat	7.579 g.	18.11 g.
Polyunsaturated Fat	2.669 g.	6.579 g.
Monounsaturated Fat	2.152 g.	4.672 g.
Saturated Fat	1.201 g.	5.001 g.
Cholesterol	0.000 mg.	24.60 mg.
Sodium	501.0 mg.; 23% USRDA	651.0 mg.; 30% USRDA
Iron	8.680 mg.; 48% USRDA	5.040 mg.; 28% USRDA
Calcium	184.4 mg.; 23% USRDA	298.4 mg.; 37% USRDA
Fiber	12.11 g.	10.94 g.

Nondairy Option
Diabetic Exchanges:
Milk: 0.0; Veg.: 2.2; Fruit: 0.0
Bread: 4.5; Meat: 0.8; Fat: 1.0

Dairy Option
Diabetic Exchanges:
Milk: 0.0; Veg.: 2.0; Fruit: 0.0
Bread: 4.4; Meat: 1.3; Fat: 3.3

LUNCHEONS

*G*ORGEOUS sunsets, narrow winding streets, pastel houses, soft white sand—these are the things that come to mind when you think of the towns and villages that nestle in the mountains along the Mediterranean Sea. The light, the water, the mountains, and the sky combine to produce one of nature's stunningly gorgeous spots.

The food is appealing too. Wild herbs blend with the earthy flavors of garlic, lentils, and garbanzo beans. Fresh, crisp vegetables contrast with the special tang of tahini—a paste made from olive oil and toasted sesame seeds.

You can make the pita bread ahead of time—and be sure to make a lot. This versatile bread can be used in many ways. Keep it in the freezer. Make the Falafels ahead too, if you want, and freeze them. You can also make the Tomato Lentil Deluxe Soup the day ahead, along with the Tahini Dressing and Hummous Dip.

◀ *Pungent garlic, crunchy pita bread, and a big tureen of hearty soup set the stage for a Mediterranean feast.*

43

TACO FROM MOROCCO
(PITA BREAD WITH FALAFELS)
Serves 1

- 1 **piece pita bread (see recipe in Greek Luncheon)**
- 2 to 3 **Falafels (see recipe following)**
- ¼ to ½ **cup shredded lettuce or ¼-½ cup alfalfa sprouts**
- ⅛ to ¼ **cup chopped tomatoes**
- 1 **tablespoon sliced green onion**
- 2 **tablespoons grated mozzarella cheese or Nondairy Pimento Cheese (see Variations section)**
- 1 to 2 **tablespoons Tahini Dressing (see recipe following)**

1. Prepare pita bread, Falafels, and Tahini Dressing.
2. Place Falafels in bottom of pita bread. Add lettuce or sprouts, tomatoes, green onions, and cheese. Drizzle with Tahini Dressing. Serve.

Makes 1 pita sandwich.

FALAFELS
Serves 8-10

- 3 **cups cooked garbanzo beans (chick peas)**
- ¼ **cup liquid from cooked beans**
- ¼ **cup wheat germ**
- 1 **small onion, finely chopped**
- 2 **garlic cloves, minced**
- 4 **tablespoons chopped fresh parsley, chopped**
- ¼ **cup sesame seeds**
- ¼ **teaspoon basil**
- ¼ **teaspoon oregano**
- 1 **teaspoon cumin**
- 1 **teaspoon chili powder (see Variations section for substitute)**
- ¼ **cup lemon juice**
- ¾ **cup cracker crumbs or wheat germ**

1. Place garbanzo beans and liquid into a blender and puree. Put bean mixture in a large bowl and add all other ingredients except the cracker crumbs or wheat germ. Mix well. Stir in just enough cracker crumbs or wheat germ so the mixture will hold together.
2. With hands, roll mixture into balls 1½-inches in diameter. Arrange balls on a cookie sheet and bake in a preheated oven at 400° F for 20-30 minutes. Turn occasionally during baking to brown evenly.
3. Serve in pita bread or as an appetizer with Tahini Dressing.

TAHINI DRESSING
Serves 14-28

- 1 **cup purchased tahini (sesame seed paste) or Homemade Tahini (recipe following)**
- ½ **cup water**
- ¼ to ½ **cup plain yogurt or Nondairy Tofu Sour Cream (see Variations section)**
- 2 **tablespoons lemon juice**
- 3 **cloves fresh garlic, crushed**

1. Blend all ingredients together in a blender until smooth. Serve.
   Note: Nutrition analysis is based on 1-tablespoon servings.

Makes 1¾ cups or 14 2-tablespoon servings or 28 1-tablespoon servings.

HOMEMADE TAHINI

- 2 **cups sesame seeds**
- ¼ **cup olive oil or other vegetable oil**

1. Place seeds in a blender or nut grinder and grind to a fine powder. Add oil slowly, blending constantly, until mixture reaches the consistency of peanut butter.
2. Use in tahini dressing recipe or as a butter or dip.

Makes about 1 cup or 16 1-tablespoon servings.

TOMATO LENTIL DELUXE SOUP
Serves 8-10

   8 ounces dry lentils
   4 cups water (add more if you prefer thinner soup)
   1 medium onion, chopped
   3 potatoes, cubed
   2 to 3 carrots, sliced
   1 bay leaf, whole
   1 to 2 teaspoons dried basil
   1 teaspoon dried oregano
   2 garlic cloves, minced or 1 teaspoon garlic powder
1½ cups cooked tomatoes, optional
   ½ cup chopped spinach, optional
      Salt to taste, optional

1. Rinse lentils and place in 5- to 6-quart pot with water, onions, potatoes, carrots, and seasonings.

2. Bring to a boil. Lower heat and let simmer, covered, 45 minutes to 1 hour, or until lentils are very soft and vegetables are tender.

3. Add tomatoes if desired, breaking apart large pieces with spoon. Add spinach, if desired. Simmer 10-15 minutes. Add salt to taste, if desired.

Note: If you're following a low-salt diet, replace salt with garlic powder to desired taste. Celery flakes also add a nice taste.

4. Serve. Soup will be quite thick. If you prefer a thinner consistency, add more water or tomato juice.

Makes about 10 cups.

GARLIC-FLAVORED PITA CHIPS
Serves 6-8

(See recipe for Cheese and Garlic Toasted Pita Chips in the Greek Luncheon and delete cheese.)

Note: Nutrition analysis for menu is based on 4 large pita chips per serving.

HUMMOUS DIP
Serves 12-24

   1 can (15 ounces) garbanzos, including liquid
   ¼ cup purchased tahini (sesame paste) or Homemade Tahini (see recipe in this menu)
   4 tablespoons lemon juice
   2 large garlic cloves, cut in thirds
   ¼ teaspoon cumin
      Salt to taste, optional
      Olive oil or chopped fresh parsley to garnish, optional

1. Drain garbanzos, reserving liquid. Put garbanzos into a blender or food processor. Add tahini, lemon juice, garlic, cumin, and ¼ cup garbanzo liquid.

2. Blend or process slowly, adding more garbanzo liquid if needed, until mixture is smooth and the consistency of heavy batter. Season to taste with salt if desired.

3. Garnish with olive oil drizzled over top or sprinkle with chopped parsley. Serve as a dip for garlic toasted pita chips.

Note: Nutrition analysis is based on 1-tablespoon servings.

Makes about 1½ cups or 12 2-tablespoon servings or 24 1-tablespoon servings.

NUTRITIONAL ANALYSIS FOR MENU:
Luncheon on the Med
Analysis based on 1 serving of each recipe listed in menu.
For individual recipe analysis, see Appendix.

	Nondairy Option	Dairy Option
Calories	527 kcal.	576 kcal.
Protein	24.07 g.; 55% USRDA	30.37 g.; 69% USRDA
Carbohydrate	81.02 g.	78.92 g.
Total Fat	15.38 g.	18.68 g.
Polyunsaturated Fat	5.193 g.	5.143 g.
Monounsaturated Fat	5.940 g.	6.700 g.
Saturated Fat	2.163 g.	4.863 g.
Cholesterol	0.000 mg.	16.10 mg.
Sodium	443.2 mg.; 20% USRDA	524.2 mg.; 24% USRDA
Iron	9.972 mg.; 55% USRDA	9.482 mg.; 53% USRDA
Calcium	290.5 mg.; 36% USRDA	480.5 mg.; 60% USRDA
Fiber	17.18 g.	16.34 g.

Nondairy Option	Dairy Option
Diabetic Exchanges:	Diabetic Exchanges:
Milk: 0.0; Veg.: 1.2; Fruit: 0.2	Milk: 0.0; Veg.: 1.2; Fruit: 0.2
Bread: 4.6; Meat: 0.8; Fat: 3.3	Bread: 4.4; Meat: 1.6; Fat: 3.633

LUNCHEONS

▶ Greek Luncheon
▶ The Better Burger and Fries
▶ Luncheon on the Med
▶ **Finnish Summer Delight**

◀ The simple designs of glass and pewter, the rich warm glow of wood, and the strong colors of the linens create a Scandinavian spirit for this meal from Finland.

*S*PARKLING *blue lakes, finally free of ice, sloping green hills thick with wild-flowers, and gardens full of delicious fresh vegetables mark the arrival of summer in Finland. After a long, cold, snowy winter, the Finns delight in summer's warmth and bounty. This international luncheon menu focuses on summer's most tender offerings. For the main dish, baby vegetables, cooked just enough to enhance their summery flavor, nestle in a light, low-calorie, nondairy, creamy soup. An assortment of delicately decorated open-faced sandwiches complement the main dish. Add the delicious Apricot Wedges for the finale, and you have a luncheon that's marvelous to look at, delightful to eat, and healthy, too.*

FINNISH SUMMER SOUP
Serves 6-8

- 2 cups water
- 4 to 6 small thin-skinned potatoes, peeled and halved
- 6 small boiling onions or 6 green onions with tops, cut in 3-inch lengths
- 12 very small baby carrots or 1 8-ounce package frozen whole baby carrots
- ½ pound fresh young green beans, cut in 1-inch lengths, or 1 9-ounce package frozen cut green beans
- 2 teaspoons garlic powder
- 1 to 2 teaspoons basil, optional
- 2 tablespoons margarine
- 2 cups fresh, shelled, tiny green peas or 1 10-ounce package frozen tiny green peas
- 2 cups skimmed evaporated milk or nondairy Cashew Rice Cream (see Variations section)
- 3 tablespoons all-purpose flour
  Salt to taste, optional

1. Heat water to boiling in wide 5-quart pan; add potatoes. Reduce heat; cover and simmer for 5-8 minutes.

2. Add onions, carrots, green beans, and garlic powder. Add basil, if desired; Add margarine; simmer for 8-10 minutes more.

3. Add peas and cook for another 2 minutes or until vegetables are crisp-tender.

4. In a small bowl, stir together evaporated milk or Cashew Rice Cream and flour until smooth. (If using Cashew Rice Cream the cream may be thick enough on its own to add to soup or may require less added flour, depending on how thick you like your soup.)

5. Stir milk and flour mixture into simmering vegetables. Cook, stirring, until soup is slightly thickened (about 5 minutes).

Makes about 8 cups.

SUNSHINE OPEN-FACED SANDWICHES
Serves 1-2

- 1 slice bread of your choice, halved
- 1 teaspoon Dilly Delight Dressing (see Variations section) or low-fat mayonnaise
- 2 leaves fresh spinach
- 1 ounce sliced or grated mozzarella cheese or Nondairy Pimento Cheese (see Variations section), optional
- 4 large mushroom slices (low-fat option) or 6-8 avocado slices
- 6 to 8 thin tomato wedges
- 2 tablespoons alfalfa sprouts to garnish

1. Place on each half of bread ½ teaspoon Dilly Delight Dressing, and 1 leaf of spinach. Add 1 ounce cheese if desired.
Note: Dilly Delight Dressing is the low-fat option for this recipe and is included in nutrition analysis.

2. Arrange vegetables on sandwich, alternating mushroom slices or avocado slices with tomato slices.

3. Garnish with 1 tablespoon sprouts.
Note: Nutrition analysis is based on low-fat options and on 1 sandwich per serving.

Makes 2 small sandwiches.

CHEESE DELIGHT OPEN-FACED SANDWICH

Serves 1-2

    1 slice of rye bread or other bread of choice, halved
    1 teaspoon Dilly Delight Dressing (see Variations section) or low-fat mayonnaise
    1 1-ounce slice mozzarella cheese or 2 tablespoons Nondairy Pimento Cheese (see Variations section)
    8 cucumbers, thinly sliced
    2 to 3 cherry tomatoes, sliced green onion tops, sliced, or chives, chopped, to garnish

    1. On each half slice of bread place ½ teaspoon Dilly Delight Dressing or mayonnaise, 1 ounce cheese, 4 slices of cucumbers overlapping, and vary every other one with tomato slices.
    Note: Nutrition analysis is based on low-fat option of Dilly Delight dressing, and 1 sandwich per serving.
    2. Garnish with sliced green onion tops or chopped chives.

APRICOT WEDGES

Serves 15-20

    1½ cups whole-wheat flour
    1½ cups rolled oats
    ½ teaspoon salt
    ¾ cup soft margarine
    ½ cup unsweetened coconut
    ½ cup chopped nuts
    4 cups dried apricots
    2 cups frozen apple juice concentrate
    2 teaspoons vanilla
    ¼ teaspoon salt, optional

    1. Soak apricots several hours in the apple juice concentrate, or until fruit is soft; drain and save liquid. (You may also cook apricots in apple juice concentrate until soft.)
    2. Whiz apricots in blender with vanilla. Add salt, if desired. Add the reserved apple juice concentrate in small amounts, using only enough to operate blender.

    3. In separate bowl, mix together flour, oats, salt, margarine, coconut, and nuts.
    4. Pat half of crumb mixture firmly into lightly oiled 10-inch circular cake pan. Add apricot mixture. Then top with remaining crumb mixture. Pat down well.
    5. Bake at 350° F for 25-30 minutes. Let cool and cut into wedges. Serve. Freezes well.

Makes about 20 1-inch wedges.

NUTRITIONAL ANALYSIS FOR MENU:
Finnish Summer Delight
Analysis based on 1 serving of each recipe listed in menu. For individual recipe analysis, see Appendix.

	Nondairy Option	Dairy Option
Calories	506 kcal.	569 kcal.
Protein	13.64 g.; 31% USRDA	18.69 g.; 42% USRDA
Carbohydrate	78.49 g.	77.28 g.
Total Fat	18.39 g.	23.17 g.
Polyunsaturated Fat	4.064 g.	4.786 g.
Monounsaturated Fat	8.546 g.	9.675 g.
Saturated Fat	3.365 g.	6.240 g.
Cholesterol	0.000 mg.	17.33 mg.
Sodium	517.0 mg.; 24% USRDA	618.0 mg.; 28% USRDA
Iron	6.170 mg.; 34% USRDA	5.098 mg.; 28% USRDA
Calcium	121.9 mg.; 15% USRDA	288.5 mg.; 36% USRDA
Fiber	10.52 g.	9.280 g.

Nondairy Option	Dairy Option
Diabetic Exchanges:	Diabetic Exchanges:
Milk: 0.0; Veg.: 2.1; Fruit: 1.4	Milk: 0.0; Veg.: 1.9; Fruit: 1.4
Bread: 2.8; Meat: 0.5; Fat: 3.6	Bread: 2.8; Meat: 1.4; Fat: 4.3

▶Italian at Its Best
▶Country Time Family Supper
▶Dinner Fresh From the Garden
▶La Fiesta Grande

*P*ASTA, *contrary to what many people think, is neither fattening nor high in cholesterol. It's those rich sauces that can add calories and wreak havoc with your waistline. This dinner evokes the spirit of Italian cooking at its very best—with healthful sauces and vegetable accompaniments for the pasta, crunchy, garlicky breadsticks, and a beautiful salad. The whole thing is quick and easy—just the thing for when you don't have much time to cook.*

Make the Italian Breadsticks ahead and freeze them. Make the Italian Sauce ahead, too, and keep it in the freezer. A quick trip to the microwave, and it is ready to serve at a moment's notice.

At mealtime, cook the pasta and vegetables, and heat the sauce. Prepare and stuff the mushrooms, toss the salad, and warm the breadsticks.

◀ *The timeless beauty of marble makes an attractive background for this classic Italian menu.*

STUFFED MUSHROOMS WITH GARLIC AND PARSLEY

Serves 8-12

- 12 large fresh mushrooms
- 1 tablespoon finely chopped lemon peel, optional
- 2 tablespoons fresh lemon juice, strained
  Salt to taste, optional
- 2 tablespoons margarine
- 2 garlic cloves, finely chopped
- ½ cup chopped fresh parsley
- 6 tablespoons fresh bread crumbs
- 4 tablespoons imitation sour cream or Nondairy Tofu Sour Cream, optional (see recipe in Variations section). Try recipe with or without any sour cream. Each way makes a different, delicious filling.

1. Carefully remove stem from each mushroom; if part of stem is still attached to cap, cut it away carefully with a small paring knife. To clean mushrooms, wipe each mushroom cap with a damp towel; do not get mushrooms too wet.

2. Preheat oven to 375° F. Arrange the mushrooms on a tray, concave side up, and lightly sprinkle each mushroom cap with lemon juice and lemon peel. Season with salt to taste, if desired.

3. Melt margarine in a skillet over medium-high heat, add the garlic, and sauté 1-2 minutes. Be sure garlic does not brown. Remove from heat and add parsley, bread crumbs, salt to taste if desired, and sour cream if desired. Toss or stir well. (If you use sour cream or nondairy sour cream, the mixture will have a thick consistency; without sour cream, the mixture will be crumbly and just a bit moist. Both ways are great!)

4. Fill each cap with the filling mixture. Handling carefully, arrange the filled mushrooms on an oiled or Pam-sprayed cookie sheet, filling side up. Bake for 15 minutes, watching carefully for the last few minutes of baking; the mushroom caps should stay firm. Overbaking will cause them to fall apart.

Makes 12 large stuffed mushrooms.

PASTA PRIMAVERA WITH ITALIAN SAUCE

Serves 6

- 1 16-ounce package of noodles, cooked according to package directions, to make 8 cups pasta. (Choose any pasta, such as spaghetti, fettuccine, bow or spiral noodles, etc.)
- 4 to 6 cups Italian Sauce (see recipe following)
- 2 small zucchini, sliced
- 2 small yellow summer squash, sliced
- 1 large onion, sliced into thin circles
- 2 cups fresh broccoli flowerets, bite-size
- 2 cups fresh cauliflower flowerets, bite-size
- 4 to 6 fresh carrots, cut into julienne slices
- 8 to 10 fresh mushrooms, sliced
  Parmesan cheese, optional, or Nondairy Parmesan Cheese (see Variations section) to garnish

1. Prepare pasta and Italian Sauce.

2. Choose any combination of vegetables you like. Place all the vegetables in a steamer and cook until crisp-tender, about 10-15 minutes. (Or microwave in a covered casserole in a small amount of water just until crisp-tender.

3. On serving platter or individual plates, place layer of pasta, layer of sauce, and top with steamed vegetables. Garnish with Parmesan cheese, if desired. Serve.

ITALIAN SAUCE
Serves 10-12

2 quarts canned tomatoes
3 6-ounce cans tomato paste
1 green pepper, halved or chopped
2 teaspoons oregano
2 teaspoons sweet basil
6 garlic cloves, minced
2 teaspoons onion powder
1 bay leaf
2 teaspoons sugar or honey
1 teaspoon lemon juice

1. Combine all ingredients in large pan. (Use whole green pepper halves and remove them later, or if you prefer, chop green peppers fine.) Bring to a gentle simmer over medium heat. Let simmer a minimum of 1 hour. The longer the sauce simmers, the better the flavor.

2. When cooking is completed, remove bay leaf and green pepper halves, if necessary. This sauce freezes well.

Makes 2½ quarts.

VEGETABLE BOUQUET WITH CREAMY BASIL DRESSING
Serves 8

1 small bunch of green leafy lettuce
1½ cups grated carrots
2 tomatoes, cut in wedges
8 fresh mushrooms, sliced
8 radishes, sliced, optional
1 cucumber, sliced
2 cups alfalfa sprouts, optional
Sunflower seeds to garnish, optional
¾ cup Nondairy Creamy Basil Dressing (see Variations section) or dressing of choice

1. Wash and prepare vegetables. Pat lettuce leaves dry with paper towel.
2. On large platter, arrange a layer of lettuce leaves with leafy edge facing out. Sprinkle grated carrots over top, and arrange tomato wedges, mushrooms, radishes (if desired), and cucumbers in a decorative

manner. Top with sprigs of sprouts or sunflower seeds, if desired. Drizzle dressing over top and chill until serving time.

ITALIAN BREADSTICKS
Serves 12-16

2 to 2¼ cups whole-wheat flour
1 package active dry yeast
4 teaspoons whole-wheat gluten flour
1½ teaspoons salt
¾ cup warm water
2 tablespoons olive or vegetable oil
1 tablespoon honey
2 to 3 garlic cloves, minced, optional
1 egg white or ¼ cup tofu, blended smooth
1 egg white for brushing on bread sticks, optional

Toppings

Parmesan cheese or Nondairy Parmesan Cheese (see Variations section), garlic powder, or salt

1. In large mixing bowl, combine 1 cup flour, yeast, whole-wheat gluten flour, and salt.
2. In separate bowl, combine ¾ cup warm water (110° F), oil, honey, and 1 egg white or blended tofu. (Be sure egg white or tofu is at room temperature.) Add garlic cloves if desired.
3. Add liquid mixture to dry mixture in mixing bowl. Beat at low speed with electric mixer for ½ minute, scraping bowl. Beat another 3 minutes at high speed.
4. By hand, stir in just enough remaining flour to make a soft dough. (Too much flour will make a heavier bread.)
5. Turn out onto lightly floured surface; knead till smooth and elastic (about 5-8 minutes). Shape into a ball. Place in lightly oiled bowl; turn once to oil top of dough. Cover; refrigerate 3 to 4 hours or overnight. (Dough may also be frozen at this point.)
6. When ready to bake, turn dough out onto a very lightly floured surface and divide it into 16 equal parts. Cover with towel; let rest 10 minutes. Then roll each piece of dough with your hands to form a pencil-like rope 10 to 12 inches long and ½ inch in di-

ameter. Smooth each rope as you work. Place ropes 2 inches apart on oiled or Pam-sprayed baking sheet.

7. Add 1 tablespoon water to egg white; beat until frothy. Using pastry brush, brush egg mixture over dough. (This step is optional, but it gives the bread an attractive shiny finish, and helps the Parmesan cheese, garlic, or salt to stick to the top.)

8. Let rise in warm place till double in size (45-60 minutes). (Because this dough was refrigerated during first rising stage, the second rising will take a little longer than usual.)

9. Brush again with egg mixture; sprinkle with topping of choice, if desired. Bake at 425° F in preheated oven for about 10 minutes. Be careful not to overbake. Overbaking makes breadsticks hard.

10. Breadsticks are best when served warm. To reheat with a just-baked flavor, place bread sticks or any rolls in a paper bag, sprinkle outside of bag with water, and fold the opening closed. Warm the rolls at 325° F until heated through, about 10 minutes. If using microwave, follow same directions but warm at medium-high temperature for about 1 minute, more or less, depending on amount of sticks being warmed. Do not overheat in microwave. It causes tough bread.

Makes 14-16 sticks.

NUTRITIONAL ANALYSIS FOR MENU:
Italian at Its Best
Analysis based on 1 serving of each recipe listed in menu. For individual recipe analysis, see Appendix.

	Nondairy Option
Calories	511 kcal.
Protein	19.35 g.; 44% USRDA
Carbohydrate	84.72 g.
Total Fat	14.17 g.
Polyunsaturated Fat	2.783 g.
Monounsaturated Fat	6.747 g.
Saturated Fat	1.890 g.
Cholesterol	0.000 mg.
Sodium	361.7 mg.; 16% USRDA
Iron	8.641 mg.; 48% USRDA
Calcium	203.4 mg.; 25% USRDA
Fiber	11.92 g.

Nondairy Option
Diabetic Exchanges:
Milk: 0.0; Veg.: 4.5; Fruit: 0.1
Bread: 3.8; Meat: 0.4; Fat: 2.1

▶Italian at Its Best
▶**Country Time Family Supper**
▶Dinner Fresh From the Garden
▶La Fiesta Grande

*P*ICTURE *a snowy afternoon on a farm. The farmer and his sons are finishing the chores. Inside the farmhouse, the farmer's wife bends over a black iron kettle, hung over an open fire. Fragrant steam rises from the stew.*

This menu is based on that kind of old-fashioned hearty country supper. Serve it on one of those rare evenings when the whole family is at home.

Bake the Herb Cheese Rosette Rolls ahead, if you like, and freeze them in sealed containers to preserve their fresh-baked flavor. Make the Vegetable Pot Pie filling and the crust the day before. Wrap the unbaked crust in plastic wrap and refrigerate it, ready to be rolled out and placed over the filling just before baking. Make the salad dressing in the food processor or blender ahead of time also.

For final preparation, assemble the pot pie and bake, prepare and toss the salad with the dressing just before serving, and warm the rolls. You have created an old-fashioned family supper, the kind memories are made of. (And aren't you thankful for your modern stove?)

◀ *A roaring fire and wholesome country-style food—the perfect combination for a winter evening at home with the family.*

VEGETABLE POT PIE

Serves 6-8

        4 raw potatoes, cubed
        4 carrots, sliced
        3 tablespoons vegetable oil
        1 large onion, chopped
     1¼ cups (10 ounces) firm tofu, cut in
           ¾-inch cubes
        2 rounded tablespoons flour
        1 cup water
        4 tablespoons light soy sauce
        1 package dark-brown George Wash-
           ington Broth or 1 package beef
           broth prepared with vegetable fat
        1 cup frozen peas
        1 oil-free biscuit-like pot pie crust
           (low-fat option, see recipe follow-
           ing) or traditional pot pie crust
           (recipe following)

1. Prepare potatoes and carrots. Place in large pot and add water to just cover vegetables. Cook just until tender. Set aside. (Do not drain.)
2. Simmer onions in oil, add tofu cubes and brown lightly. Sprinkle with flour. Add water, broth mix, and soy sauce.
3. Add onion/tofu mixture to potatoes and carrots with water in which they were cooked. Add peas.
4. Simmer until stew is slightly thickened. For pot pie, place stew in a 9″ deep-dish pie pan, a 10-inch cast-iron skillet, or individual-serving-size ovenproof soup bowls.
5. Prepare the crust of your choice and place on top of vegetable stew filling, following directions in crust recipe. Cut steam vents in crust. (Nutrition analysis based on oil-free crust.)
6. Bake in preheated 375° F oven for about 30-40 minutes (depending on size of container), or until crust is golden brown and filling begins to bubble. (If filling is cold before baking, it may take it as long as 50 minutes to begin bubbling.) Serve.

OIL-FREE BISCUIT-LIKE POT PIE CRUST

     1½ cups warm water
        1 tablespoon honey
        1 package active dry yeast
        1 cup fine cornmeal
        1 cup all-purpose flour
     1⅓ cup whole-wheat flour
        5 tablespoons whole-wheat gluten
           flour
        ½ teaspoon salt

1. Mix ½ cup of the warm water with the honey; sprinkle with yeast and set aside.
2. In a large bowl, mix flours and salt. Add dissolved yeast and the additional 1 cup warm water and mix well to form dough.
3. Place dough on floured board and knead lightly. (Overkneading at this point will make dough too elastic to roll out thin.)
4. With a lightly floured rolling pin, roll dough out ¼-inch thick in a circle 2 inches wider than pie pan or individual serving soup bowls. Or if you prefer, cut rolled-out dough into shapes with cookie cutter. (Dough thickness will double when it rises, so make it as thin as possible.)
5. Lay rolled-out dough on top of vegetable stew filling. Seal edges, and flute if desired. Or, if you have cut dough into shapes, arrange them on top of vegetable stew. Continue with Vegetable Pot Pie recipe step 6.

Makes 1 crust.

RASPBERRY WALNUT VEGETABLE SALAD

Serves 6-8

    2 medium-sized cucumbers, thinly
       sliced
    2 medium-sized tomatoes, cubed
    3 stalks celery, very thinly sliced
    3 carrots, thinly sliced
  ½ to 1 cup walnuts
    2 garlic cloves, minced
    1 teaspoon coriander
    8 tablespoons cold water
    4 tablespoons lemon juice
    2 tablespoons raspberry juice, op-
       tional
    4 tablespoons chopped fresh parsley
    2 tablespoons minced onion
    6 large leaves romaine lettuce, or 12
       large leaves spinach
       Parsley sprigs to garnish

1. In a large bowl, combine cucumbers, tomatoes, celery, and carrots. Set aside and chill.
2. In a food processor or blender, process the walnuts, garlic, and coriander to a paste. Add the water, lemon juice, and raspberry juice (if desired), and blend until smooth. (Rasberrry juice adds a great taste and a nice pink color to dressing, but the salad is also quite good without it.) Stir in parsley and onion.
3. Pour dressing over chilled vegetables (use from half to all of the dressing, as desired); mix gently but thoroughly.
4. To serve, mound the salad on beds of romaine or spinach leaves; garnish with parsley sprigs.

HERB CHEESE ROSETTE ROLLS

Serves 20-24

  1½ cups whole-wheat flour
  1½ cups all-purpose flour
    2 tablespoons whole-wheat gluten
       flour
   ¼ cup wheat germ
    1 package active dry yeast
   ½ cup warm water (about 110° F)
  1½ tablespoons honey
  1½ teaspoons salt
   ½ cup warm water (about 110° F)
  2½ tablespoons margarine, melted
    2 egg whites, lightly beaten, or ⅓ cup
       tofu, blended smooth
   ½ teaspoon oregano
   ½ teaspoon basil
   ¼ teaspoon savory leaves
   ¼ teaspoon thyme leaves
   ½ teaspoon garlic powder
   ⅛ cup instant toasted onions
   ⅛ cup Parmesan cheese or Nondairy
       Parmesan Cheese (see Variations
       section)

1. In a bowl, mix together flours and wheat germ.
2. In a large bowl, dissolve yeast in ½ cup warm water. Add honey, salt, additional warm water, melted margarine, and tofu or egg whites (Be sure tofu or egg whites are at room temperature.) Mix in oregano, basil, savory, thyme, garlic powder, instant onions, and Parmesan cheese.
3. Add 1½ cups of flour mixture to liquid and beat until elastic (about 5 minutes at medium speed if using electric mixer.)
4. With heavy-duty mixer, bread maker, or with a wooden spoon, gradually beat in remaining flour mixture. Dough should be soft, but not too sticky to knead; add additional all-purpose flour if necessary to prevent sticking.
5. Turn dough out onto a floured board and knead just until smooth (about 5 minutes).
6. Divide dough into 3 equal pieces. Divide each third into eight pieces. On a lightly floured surface, use your hands to roll each

piece into a pencil-like strand, 12 inches long. Tie a loose knot in center of strand, leaving two long ends. Tuck top end under roll. Bring bottom end up and tuck into center of knot. Place rosettes 2-3 inches apart on oiled baking sheet. Cover with towel and let rise until doubled in size (about 30-40 minutes).

7. Bake in preheated 400° F oven for about 10-12 minutes or until lightly browned. (Don't overbake, or rolls will be hard.) Remove from pans and cool on rack.

Makes about 24 rolls.

NUTRITIONAL ANALYSIS FOR MENU:
Country Time Family Supper
Analysis based on 1 serving of each recipe listed in menu. For individual recipe analysis, see Appendix.

	Nondairy Option	Dairy Option
Calories	544 kcal.	546 kcal.
Protein	21.02 g.; 48% USRDA	20.77 g.; 47% USRDA
Carbohydrate	89.86 g.	89.56 g.
Total Fat	13.73 g.	14.19 g.
Polyunsaturated Fat	4.678 g.	4.596 g.
Monounsaturated Fat	5.472 g.	5.839 g.
Saturated Fat	1.808 g.	1.963 g.
Cholesterol	0.000 mg.	0.429 mg.
Sodium	711.0 mg.; 32% USRDA	733.0 mg.; 33% USRDA
Iron	9.010 mg.; 50% USRDA	8.535 mg.; 47% USRDA
Calcium	171.8 mg.; 21% USRDA	168.0 mg.; 21% USRDA
Fiber	10.47 g.	10.42 g.

Nondairy Option
Diabetic Exchanges:
Milk: 0.0; Veg.: 2.4; Fruit: 0.0
Bread: 4.4; Meat: 1.0; Fat: 2.1

Dairy Option
Diabetic Exchanges:
Milk: 0.0; Veg.: 2.4; Fruit: 0.0
Bread: 4.4; Meat: 1.0; Fat: 2.2

DINNERS

► Italian at Its Best
► Country Time Family Supper
► **Dinner Fresh From the Garden**
► La Fiesta Grande

*M*AKE this dinner in the summertime, or as soon as your local fresh asparagus is available, so you can take advantage of the season's bountiful crop, brimming with garden-fresh flavor. Make sure you buy your produce while it's as fresh as possible, and use it right away. The fresher the produce, the better the flavor.

Bake the Dilly Twists ahead and freeze them if you like. Cook the artichokes ahead of time and bring them to room temperature before serving. Make the Pineapple Potato Boats the day or morning before serving and brown them just before serving. Prepare and chill the salad dressing ahead of time.

At the last minute, assemble and microwave the Vegetable Medley, toss and garnish the salad, and warm the Dilly Twists. Enjoy the delicious results of your effort with family and friends, knowing that these wonderful fresh vegetables are the healthiest foods you can serve.

◄ *Summer's bounty, arranged and displayed like fine art, needs no further decoration.*

ARTICHOKES À LA BÉARNAISE
Serves 4

- 2 artichokes
  Fresh lemon juice
- 1 teaspoon salt, optional
- 4 to 6 tablespoons nondairy Dilly Delight Dip (see Variations section) or mayonnaise mixed with 2 teaspoons fresh minced parsley, 1½ teaspoons fresh lemon juice, and onion powder to taste.
- 4 large leaves butterhead lettuce
  Lemon wedges

1. Select compact, plump artichokes with tightly closed, thick green leaves that break off crisply. With a sharp, serrated knife, cut the stem straight across so the artichoke will stand. Cut 1 inch off the top. Pull off the bottom row of leaves and, with kitchen shears, cut off spiny tips of the remaining leaves. Rinse thoroughly and dry with towel. Rub the cut edges with lemon juice to prevent discoloring. The choke (hairlike spines in the center of the artichoke) can be removed before or after cooking. To remove, spread the top leaves apart and pull out the center cluster of leaves. Then scrape out the hairy choke with a grapefruit spoon.

2. Place artichokes in a 3-quart saucepan; add 2 cups water, and salt if desired, and bring to a boil. Reduce heat to low and simmer for 40-50 minutes or until leaves pull away easily and bottom stem is soft when pricked with a fork. Remove artichokes from pan with a slotted spoon, and drain.

3. Make nondairy Dilly Delight Dip or mayonnaise dip, chill until serving time.

4. To serve, cut each artichoke in half lengthwise. Remove choke if not removed previously, and place halves on lettuce leaves. Spoon 1-2 tablespoons of the dip onto each half.

Note: Nutrition analysis is based on Dilly Delight Dip, the low-fat option.

PINEAPPLE-POTATO BOATS
Serves 6

- 3 medium baking potatoes
- 1 2½-ounce package Neufchâtel cheese or ⅓ cup Nondairy Tofu Sour Cream (see Variations Section)
- 1 to 2 teaspoons nonfat milk or soy milk
- 2 tablespoons sugar-free canned pineapple, cut into tiny pieces, with juice, skim milk, soy milk, or water
  Salt to taste, optional

1. Scrub potatoes; prick with fork. Bake in 325° F oven for 1-1¼ hours, or until done.

2. Cut potatoes in half lengthwise. Carefully scoop out insides, reserving shells. Blend Neufchâtel cheese with 1-2 teaspoons milk until smooth. Mash potatoes; blend in cheese mixture or nondairy sour cream, pineapple pieces, and salt if desired. Adding 1 teaspoon of liquid at a time, beat in enough milk or water to make potato mixture fluffy. Pile mixture into reserved potato shells.

3. Bake, in shallow baking pan, in a preheated 325° F oven 20-25 minutes. Garnish with paprika if desired.

Makes 6 potato boats.

VEGETABLE MEDLEY
Serves 6

- 6 medium-sized green onions with tops, sliced thin
- 6 to 8 tablespoons grated Parmesan cheese or Nondairy Parmesan Cheese (see Variations section)
- ¼ teaspoon dried basil
- ¼ teaspoon dried oregano
- ¼ teaspoon garlic powder
- 24 medium-sized fresh asparagus spears, trimmed
- 3 medium-sized ripe tomatoes, quartered
- 2 tablespoons water

1. Mix sliced green onions, Parmesan cheese, basil, oregano, and garlic powder in a small bowl.

2. On a 10- to 12-inch round, microwave-safe serving plate, arrange asparagus in a spoke fashion with stem ends toward edge of plate and tips overlapping in center. Place tomato quarters in a circular pattern 2 inches from edge of plate.

3. Sprinkle vegetables with water, then with the green onion mixture. Cover with vented plastic wrap. Microwave on high 5-8 minutes, rotating dish a half turn once, until vegetables are hot. Let stand covered 3-5 minutes until crisp-tender. Tilt plate and drain off liquid through vent opening. Serve immediately.

AVOCADO-ALMOND SALAD WITH APRICOT-YOGURT DRESSING

Serves 8

2 tablespoons margarine, optional
¼ to ½ cup slivered almonds
1 large head romaine lettuce, torn into bite-sized pieces
½ pound spinach, torn into bite-sized pieces
1 cup mung bean sprouts
1 to 2 avocados, each sliced into eight pieces
1 to 2 tablespoons Apricot-Yogurt Dressing (recipe following)

1. In a small skillet, sauté almonds in melted margarine; set aside to cool. (If desired, you may delete this step and use plain slivered almonds.)

2. Prepare Apricot-Yogurt Dressing, recipe following.

3. In a large salad bowl, toss romaine, spinach, and sprouts. Divide onto 8 salad plates. Place 2 avocado slices on each serving; top with Apricot-Yogurt Dressing.

4. Garnish each serving with almonds.

APRICOT-YOGURT DRESSING

Serves 16-20

1 cup plain yogurt or Nondairy Tofu Sour Cream (see Variations section)
¼ cup dried apricots, coarsely chopped
3 tablespoons safflower oil
2 tablespoons lemon juice
1 teaspoon honey
1 teaspoon onion, minced
1 teaspoon celery seed, optional
Salt to taste, optional

1. In a food processor or blender, blend yogurt and apricots until smooth. Stir in oil, lemon juice, honey, onion. Add celery seed and salt, if desired. Chill briefly before serving. Serve with avocado-almond salad.

Makes 1¼ cups or 20 1-tablespoon servings.

DILLY TWISTS

Serves 12-24

1 cup chopped onion
¼ cup water
½ cup warm water (115° F)
1½ tablespoons active dry yeast
2 tablespoons honey
½ cup additional warm water (115° F)
3 to 3½ cups whole-wheat flour
6 teaspoons whole-wheat gluten flour
2 teaspoons salt
1½ tablespoons oil, optional
¼ cup cornmeal
⅛ cup yellow yeast flakes
2 tablespoons dried dill weed

1. Sauté onions in ¼ cup water and set aside.

2. Combine ½ cup warm water, yeast, and honey, and let stand until bubbles appear.

3. In mixing bowl, beat the additional ½ cup warm water with 1 cup whole-wheat flour and the whole-wheat gluten flour for 1 minute. Add yeast mixture to the flour mixture and allow to rise until doubled in size (about 45-60 minutes).

4. Add cooked onion, salt, oil if desired, cornmeal, yeast flakes, and dillweed. Gradually add remaining whole-wheat flour, 1 cup at a time, adding just enough flour to prevent sticky dough. Dough should be soft. Knead 5 minutes.

5. Place in lightly oiled pan. Turn dough once to oil top. Cover, and let raise in warm place until doubled in size (about 45 minutes).

6. Punch down dough and divide into 2 equal parts. Round each into a ball. With a lightly floured rolling pin, roll each ball into a 14″ x 6″ rectangle. Brush with melted margarine, if desired. Fold lengthwise into a 14″ x 3″ rectangle. Cut crosswise into strips 3-inches long and 1-inch wide. Twist each strip and place 2-3 inches apart on oiled baking sheet, pressing ends down on sheet. Cover with towel, and let rise about 30-40 minutes.

7. Bake in preheated 375° F oven for 10-12 minutes or just until golden brown. (Over-baking will make the twists hard and dry.) Remove from pan and cool on racks.

8. To store: Place cooled twists in plastic bag or sealed container to preserve moistness.

9. To reheat: Place twists in paper bag, fold down top, and mist water on the outside of bag. Heat in 325° F oven for 10-12 minutes or until thoroughly warmed. To microwave, place 6 or more twists in paper bag, as prepared above, in microwave and heat at medium-high heat for about 1 minute. If warming 2-4 twists, microwave for 20 seconds. Freeze any extra twists for later use.

Note: Nutrition analysis for menu is based on 2 Dilly Twists per serving.

Makes approximately 24 Dilly Twists.

NUTRITIONAL ANALYSIS FOR MENU:
Dinner Fresh From the Garden
Analysis based on 1 serving of each recipe listed in menu.
For individual recipe analysis, see Appendix.

	Nondairy Option	Dairy Option
Calories	576 kcal.	530 kcal.
Protein	26.23 g.; 60% USRDA	24.96 g.; 57% USRDA
Carbohydrate	79.34 g.	76.11 g.
Total Fat	22.30 g.	18.70 g.
Polyunsaturated Fat	8.615 g.	4.131 g.
Monounsaturated Fat	8.721 g.	7.817 g.
Saturated Fat	2.956 g.	4.899 g.
Cholesterol	0.000 mg.	14.99 mg.
Sodium	605.7 mg.; 28% USRDA	678.6 mg.; 31% USRDA
Iron	12.06 mg.; 67% USRDA	8.590 mg.; 48% USRDA
Calcium	316.7 mg.; 40% USRDA	337.6 mg.; 42% USRDA
Fiber	15.58 g.	14.89 g.

Nondairy Option Diabetic Exchanges:	Dairy Option Diabetic Exchanges:
Milk: 0.0; Veg.: 4.7; Fruit: 0.1	Milk: 0.1; Veg.: 4.5; Fruit: 0.1
Bread: 2.8; Meat: 1.1; Fat: 4.4	Bread: 2.8; Meat: 1.2; Fat: 3.25

►Italian at Its Best
►Country Time Family Supper
►Dinner Fresh From the Garden
►**La Fiesta Grande**

*D*USTY *village streets, colorful fiestas filled with the sounds of guitars, or bustling big cities—all are typical of Mexico's incredible variety. Mexican food is varied too. With just a little thought, it can be healthful as well as festive and delicious.*

The Impossible Taco Pie is unique—the kind of dish that will make your friends ask you for the recipe. Prepare and bake it a day ahead, if you like. Then prepare the lettuce, tomato, and sour cream or Nondairy Tofu Sour Cream to arrange on top just before serving.

Make the beans and rice ahead, too. Only the Vegetable Con Queso Nachos, Chili-Tomato Sauce, and a Guacamole need to be made a few hours before serving. Just before your guests arrive, bake the Toasted Corn Tortilla Chips and mix up the Fiesta Fruit Punch, and you're ready to serve everyone's favorite Mexican meal. Ole!

◄ **Colorful pottery and an old brick patio provide an appropriate setting for this south-of-the-border feast.**

VEGETABLE CON QUESO NACHOS

Serves 6

> 3 medium-sized zucchinis, cut into ¼-inch thick slices
> 4 tablespoons green chilies, chopped
> ¾ cup low-fat mozzarella cheese, grated, or ¾ cup Nondairy Pimento Cheese (see Variations section)
> Chili-Tomato Sauce, optional (see recipe following)

1. Prepare zucchini and arrange slices in overlapping rows on an ovenproof platter. Top evenly with the chilies and cheese.
2. Place on boiler rack 4-6 inches from heat until cheese has melted (or until pimento cheese begins to bubble), about 5 minutes.
3. Serve with Chili-Tomato Sauce for dipping, if desired.

CHILI-TOMATO SAUCE

Serves 14-18

> 2 medium-sized tomatoes, peeled and chopped
> ¼ cup chopped onion
> ¼ cup chopped celery
> ¼ cup chopped green pepper
> ½ to ¾ cup minced green chilies (remove seeds for milder flavor)
> ¼ cup tomato paste
> 2 tablespoon safflower oil
> ½ teaspoon coriander
> Salt to taste, optional

1. In a food processor or blender, puree the tomatoes, onion, celery, and green pepper.
2. Transfer the pureed mixture to a medium-sized saucepan and add the remaining ingredients. (Use more chilies for a hotter sauce, less for a milder one.) Bring mixture to a boil, reduce heat, and simmer, uncovered, for 20 minutes, stirring occasionally.
3. To store: Place in covered jar and refrigerate. Serve at room temperature. This sauce is best when made a few days ahead so that the flavors have time to blend.

Makes 1 ¾ cups or 14 2-tablespoon servings.

IMPOSSIBLE TACO PIE

Serves 6-8

> 3 cups Chili Beans (see recipe following)
> 1 4-ounce can green chilies, drained and chopped
> 1½ cups yellow cornmeal
> ⅓ cup raw cashew pieces
> 2 cups water
> ½ teaspoon salt
> 1 teaspoon vanilla
> 2 tablespoons honey
> 3 cups lettuce, chopped
> 2 to 3 cups tomatoes, chopped
> Cheese or Nondairy Pimento Cheese (see Variations section)
> ½ cup sour cream or Nondairy Tofu Sour Cream (see Variations section)

1. Prepare Chili Beans, recipe following.
2. Place cornmeal, cashews, water, salt, vanilla, and honey in blender and blend until smooth. Set aside.
3. Oil (or spray with Pam) a pie plate, 10 inches in diameter by 1½ inches deep. Place Chili Beans in bottom of pie plate; sprinkle with chilies.
4. Pour cashew-cornmeal mixture over chilies. Bake in preheated 400° F oven for 25 minutes. Sprinkle with grated cheese or Nondairy Pimento Cheese (see Variations section) and bake 8-10 minutes longer. Cool 5 minutes before proceeding to next step.
5. Arrange chopped lettuce in circle around outside edge, then arrange chopped tomatoes in circle inside the lettuce circle. Place sour cream or Nondairy Tofu Sour Cream in center. Serve with side dishes of guacamole and Chili Tomato Sauce.

Makes 1 10" x 1½" taco pie.

CHILI BEANS

> 5 cups small red, pink, or pinto beans, uncooked, or 10 cups unseasoned canned beans
> 1 tablespoon salt, optional
> 2 large onions, quartered
> 1 to 3 tablespoons cumin, or to taste
> 3 garlic cloves, minced
> 2 to 3 teaspoons chili powder or Chili Powder Substitute (see Variations section)
> 1 quart canned tomatoes
> 1 green pepper, chopped
> 1 tablespoon margarine, optional

1. For uncooked beans: Soak beans overnight.
2. Cook for 2 hours in enough water to keep beans covered. If using pressure cooker, cook with pressure up for 1 hour.
3. To homemade cooked beans or 10 cups canned beans, add remaining ingredients. Simmer over low heat for several hours, stirring occasionally. (The longer the beans cook, the better their flavor.) Serve.

Makes 5 quarts.

FIESTA ENSALADA
Serves 4

> 2 jicamas, cubed
> 1 small cucumber, cubed
> 1 orange, peeled, seeded, and cubed
> 2 tablespoons lemon juice
> 1 tablespoon grated lemon rind
> Dash of ground cinnamon, or Cinnamon Substitute (see Variations section)
> 6 to 8 green leafy lettuce leaves

1. In large bowl, toss the cubed jicama, cucumber, and orange. Add the lemon rind and cinnamon; toss to coat. Cover and chill.
2. Place all lettuce leaves on large platter, or one lettuce leaf each on individual serving plates, and mound salad mixture on top. Serve.

ARROZ MEXICANO (MEXICAN RICE)
Serves 6

> 2 tablespoons safflower oil, optional
> 1 cup uncooked brown rice
> 1 cup chopped tomatoes
> 2 tablespoons tomato sauce or catsup
> 1 small onion, chopped
> 2 cloves garlic, minced
> 2⅓ cups water
> 1 teaspoon dried parsley
> ⅛ teaspoon thyme
> ½ teaspoon basil
> ½ teaspoon light soy sauce
> 1 cup diced, cooked carrots, optional
> ½ cup cooked peas, optional
> 1 tablespoon chopped green chilies
> 1 tablespoon fresh parsley, chopped

1. Heat the oil in large saucepan; add the rice and stir until rice is coated with the oil. (Although this step is optional, it helps to prevent sticky rice.)
2. In a food processor or blender, process the tomatoes, tomato sauce, or catsup, onion, garlic, ⅓ cup water, and dried parsley, thyme, basil, and soy sauce until smooth. Stir into the rice in large saucepan.
3. Add the remaining water; cover, and cook over medium heat until the liquid has been absorbed and the rice is tender, about 45 minutes.
4. Stir in carrots, peas, chilies, and parsley; heat through. (Adding these vegetables to rice mixture is optional. You might want to try this recipe both ways.)
5. Serve immediately; or refrigerate for 1 day if you prefer, and reheat in a saucepan on top of the stove, or in an ovenproof casserole at 350° F for 30 minutes. To microwave, place in microwave-safe casserole dish and heat on high for 10-15 minutes, stirring once, or until heated thoroughly.

Makes about 3½ cups.

GUACAMOLE
Serves 32

> 2 avocados
> 1 medium-sized tomato, finely chopped
> ½ cup low-fat, plain yogurt, optional, or Nondairy Tofu Sour Cream (see Variations section)
> ¼ cup minced onion
> 2 green chilies, minced
> 2 teaspoons lemon juice
> 1 clove garlic, minced
> Salt to taste, optional

1. Mash the avocados until very smooth, or a little chunky, as desired. Stir in the remaining ingredients. (This recipe can be made with or without yogurt or Nondairy Tofu Sour Cream. It will be different, but equally delicious either way.)
2. Cover and refrigerate at least 1 hour before serving. Serve on the side with Vegetable Con Queso Nachos, Impossible Taco Pie, or Toasted Corn Tortillas.

Makes about 2 cups or 32 1-tablespoon servings.

TOASTED CORN TORTILLA CHIPS
Serves 4-6

> 6 soft uncooked corn tortillas
> Salt to taste, optional

1. Place all 6 corn tortillas in a stack. Cut in quarters, then cut quarters in half to make 8 wedge-shaped stacks of chips.
2. Arrange chips, one layer thick, on un-oiled baking sheet. Add salt to taste, if desired. (You may brush chips lightly with oil to help salt to stay on better, but these taste great without any oil.) Bake in preheated 400° F oven for 8-10 minutes, watching carefully to avoid browning. These may also be baked for ½ hour at 250° F. Serve.

Makes about 48 chips or 6 servings of 8 chips each.

FIESTA FRUIT PUNCH
Serves 10

> 1 6-ounce can frozen orange juice concentrate
> 1 6-ounce can frozen lemonade concentrate
> 4½ cups water
> 2 cups canned, unsweetened peaches, undrained
> 1 to 2 tablespoons Coco Lopez, cream of coconut, or about ½ teaspoon coconut extract, to taste
> 2 cups club soda or 2 cups additional water

1. Mix juice concentrates with 4½ cups water.
2. Puree peaches in blender, add cream of coconut or coconut extract.
3. Add peaches to orange-lemon juice mixture along with additional water and store in refrigerator until ready to serve. If using club soda, add it just before serving to preserve the bubbles.

Makes 10 cups or 10 8-ounce servings.

NUTRITIONAL ANALYSIS FOR MENU:
La Fiesta Grande
Analysis based on 1 serving of each recipe listed in menu. For individual recipe analysis, see Appendix.

	Nondairy Option	Dairy Option
Calories	562 kcal.	601 kcal.
Protein	15.05 g.; 34% USRDA	20.27 g.; 46% USRDA
Carbohydrate	96.85 g.	93.86 g.
Total Fat	16.19 g.	20.06 g.
Polyunsaturated Fat	6.219 g.	5.091 g.
Monounsaturated Fat	4.571 g.	5.401 g.
Saturated Fat	2.013 g.	6.241 g.
Cholesterol	0.000 mg.	22.58 mg.
Sodium	391.9 mg.; 18% USRDA	449.1 mg.; 20% USRDA
Iron	5.971 mg.; 33% USRDA	4.790 mg.; 27% USRDA
Calcium	207.9 mg.; 26% USRDA	388.9 mg.; 49% USRDA
Fiber	11.38 g.	10.44 g.

Nondairy Option	Dairy Option
Diabetic Exchanges:	Diabetic Exchanges:
Milk: 0.0; Veg.: 3.0; Fruit: 1.6	Milk: 0.1; Veg.: 3.0; Fruit: 1.6
Bread: 3.2; Meat: 0.6; Fat: 3.1	Bread: 3.1; Meat: 1.2; Fat: 3.7

SPECIAL OCCASIONS

▶ **Anniversary Dinner for Two**
▶ Stars and Stripes Barbecue
▶ Tailgate Picnic
▶ Valentine Candlelight Dinner
▶ New Year's Eve Pizza Party
▶ Jingle Bells Buffet

*F*IRELIGHT and crystal, snowy linen and your best china. A Chopin sonata playing softly in the background. The children all tucked into their beds. This is going to be a special anniversary dinner just for the two of you, and you're pulling out all the stops to make it perfect. And it's good to know, when you're cooking for that very special person, that everything you're serving is low in calories, free of cholesterol, and heart-healthy.

The delicious Spinach-stuffed Lasagna Swirls provide the beautiful main course for the celebration. The Vegetable Bundles add a festive, gift-wrapped touch of the gourmet (and they give the appearance that you slaved over them for hours, even though you didn't). For a perfect complement to the meal, serve light-tasting, eye-appealing Pear Sorbet With Raspberry Sauce. The recipe is found in the dessert menu.

◀ *Grandmother's silver catches the firelight, but the food is the real star of this cozy dinner party for two.*

SPINACH-STUFFED LASAGNA SWIRLS WITH ITALIAN SAUCE

Serves 6-8

> 6 **cups Italian Sauce (recipe in Italian dinner) or ready-made sauce**
> 1 **18-ounce box lasagna noodles**
>   **Nondairy Tofu Filling or Riccota Filling**

Tofu Filling

> 1 **pound (2 cups) tofu, blended or mashed**
> 2 **tablespoons olive oil**
> 1 **tablespoon fresh lemon juice**
> 1 **tablespoon honey**
> 2 **teaspoons garlic powder**
> 1 **teaspoon basil**
>   **Salt to taste, optional**

Riccota Filling

> 2 **cups cottage cheese or riccota cheese**
> 2 **egg whites, slightly beaten**
> 1 **teaspoon garlic powder**

Add to either the tofu or riccota filling:

> 1 **tablespoon olive oil or 2 tablespoons water**
> 1 **teaspoon basil**
> 1 **teaspoon oregano**
> 1 **teaspoon garlic powder**
>   **Salt to taste, optional**
> 1½ **cups chopped onions**
> 1 **10-ounce package frozen chopped spinach, thawed and drained**

1. Prepare Italian Sauce if not using prepared sauce.
2. Drop lasagna noodles into boiling water and cook for about 10 minutes until noodles are al dente or almost done.
3. Choose either tofu or ricotta filling and proceed as indicated below:
4. For tofu filling: Mash or blend tofu smooth. Blend in oil, lemon juice, honey, and garlic powder. Add salt to taste, if desired.
5. For cottage cheese filling: Mix together cottage cheese, egg whites, and garlic powder.

6. Sauté onions in oil or water.
7. Blend sautéed onions into filling mixture of your choice. Add spinach and mix well.
8. Pour 2 cups of Italian Sauce into the bottom of a 9″ x 13″ baking pan. Lay each lasagna noodle flat and spread ½ cup filling over the entire noodle. Roll noodle carefully and place, seam side down, in baking pan. Continue with remaining noodles. Cover with the rest of the sauce. Bake in a preheated 350° F oven for about 30 minutes, or until lasagna is heated thoroughly and sauce bubbles. To microwave: Cover and heat at high temperature for about 20 minutes, or until lasagna is heated thoroughly and sauce bubbles. Serve.

Makes about 14 pieces.

VEGETABLE BUNDLES

Serves 6-12

> ½ **large red bell pepper**
> 6 **snow peas**
> 1 **celery stalk**
> 1 **small zucchini**
> 12 **green beans**
> 1 **large carrot**

Marinade (Optional)

> 6 **tablespoons olive oil**
> 2 **tablespoons lemon juice**
> ½ **teaspoon garlic powder**
>   **Salt to taste, optional**
> 2 **green onions with tops**

1. Core and seed pepper and slice into ¼-inch strips. Cut strips into 2½-inch lengths. Set aside in bowl of ice water.
2. Cut snow peas and celery stalks in ¼″ x 2½″ strips. Add to bowl with pepper strips.
3. Scrub zucchini and trim ends but do not peel. Cut into strips the same size as other vegetables, discarding seedy centers. Steam zucchini in covered casserole in microwave on high setting with 1 teaspoon water until barely tender, about 3-5 minutes. Or steam in pan with steam basket over boiling water for 3-5 minutes.
4. Cut green beans and carrots into strips to match other vegetables. Steam each until tender in steam basket or microwave, and

add to ice water bowl. Drain all vegetables and pat dry with cotton towels.

5. Make marinade: Combine oil, lemon juice, and garlic powder. Add salt to taste if desired, and mix well. Toss with vegetables and marinate several hours at room temperature. (To vary recipe, omit marinade and drizzle melted margarine over vegetable bundles as garnish.)

6. Trim tops from green onions. Separate onion leaves carefully, keeping them as long as possible. (Each leaf is to wrap a 1-inch bundle of vegetables.) Drop raw onion leaves into boiling water in a large skillet. Turn off heat immediately and transfer onion leaves to cotton towel to dry.

7. Place one onion leaf on work surface. On top of it, arrange a variety of the prepared vegetables to make a bundle about 1 inch in diameter. Wrap the bundle with the onion leaf, tying carefully, or just wrap leaf tightly around bundle as far as it will stretch. Arrange bundles on a flat platter or individual serving plates. When all bundles are made, pour any excess marinade over bundles and serve. Or, if not using marinade, drizzle melted margarine over bundles and serve.

Note: Menu nutrition analysis is based on 2 bundles per serving.

Makes 12 bundles.

ITALIAN GREEN SALAD WITH POPPY SEED DRESSING
Serves 6-8

> 1 **bunch romaine lettuce**
> 1 **bunch green leaf lettuce**
> 2 **tomatoes, cut in wedges**
> ½ **green or red pepper, cut in strips**
> ½ **cup sliced cucumber (peel and halve cucumber, longways, before slicing)**
> ¼ **cup sliced green onion**
> 1 **to 2 tablespoons Poppy Seed Dressing (recipe following)**

1. Wash and dry lettuce. Tear greens in bite-sized pieces in salad bowl.

2. Add tomato wedges, green pepper strips, cucumber slices, and sliced green onion. Toss lightly. Serve with Poppy Seed Dressing.

POPPY SEED DRESSING
Serves 16-32

> ½ **small white onion, chopped**
> ½ **cup honey**
> ⅓ **cup lemon juice**
> 1 **teaspoon dry mustard, optional**
> ¾ **teaspoon salt, optional**
> 1 **cup olive oil or other vegetable oil or ½ cup oil and ½ cup water**
> 2 **tablespoons poppy seeds**

1. In blender or food processor, blend chopped onion on medium speed until onion is slushy.

2. Add honey and lemon juice to onion in blender or food processor. Add dry mustard and salt to taste, if desired.

3. With blender or food processor running on medium-high speed, slowly pour in oil, or oil/water mixture. Mixture in blender will be thick and creamy. If you use oil/water mixture, it will be slightly thinner, but still delicious.

4. Add poppy seeds and blend or process a few seconds longer, being careful to not run too long so that poppy seeds remain whole.

5. Store in refrigerator until needed. Serve chilled with Italian Green Salad or favorite salad combination.

Note: Menu nutrition analysis is based on 2 tablespoons per serving.

Makes 2 cups or 32 1-tablespoon servings or 16 2-tablespoon servings.

WHOLE-WHEAT ITALIAN BREAD

3 to 3½ cups whole-wheat flour
5 teaspoons whole-wheat gluten flour
1 tablespoon active dry yeast
1¼ cups warm water (115° F)
1 tablespoon honey
1 teaspoon salt
Yellow cornmeal
1 slightly beaten egg white, optional

1. In large mixing bowl, combine 1½ cups of flour, gluten flour, and yeast.

2. Combine warm water, honey, and salt in separate bowl.

3. Add liquid mixture to dry mixture. Beat at low speed with electric mixer for ½ minute, scraping sides of bowl constantly. Beat 3 minutes at high speed.

4. By hand, stir in remaining flour to make a very stiff dough. Turn out onto a lightly floured surface and knead until smooth and very elastic (15-20 minutes). Shape into a ball. Place dough in a lightly oiled bowl, turn once to oil surface of dough. Cover and let dough rise in a warm place till doubled in size (1-1¼ hours).

5. Punch dough down; turn out onto lightly floured surface. Cover with a towel and let rest 10 minutes.

6. With a lightly floured rolling pin, roll dough out into a 15″ x 12″ rectangle. Beginning at long side of rectangle, roll dough up tightly with your hands, pinching seam to seal well as you roll. Taper ends of loaf. Place each loaf diagonally, seam side down, on oiled baking sheet that has been sprinkled with cornmeal. With sharp knife, make diagonal cuts, 2½ inches apart and ⅛ to ¼ inch deep, across top of loaf. (You may also shape dough into round loaf or hard rolls at this point.)

7. Cover loaf with towel and let rise in warm place till doubled in size (45-60 minutes).

8. Preheat oven to 375° F. When oven is hot and bread is ready for baking, place a large shallow pan on lower rack of oven and fill with boiling water (to make a more moist loaf).

9. Add 1 tablespoon water to egg white and lightly beat. Brush over top and sides of risen loaf. (This step is optional. It gives bread a shiny, browned surface.)

10. Bake loaf for 15 minutes, brush again with egg mixture, if desired, and continue baking for 15 additional minutes or until golden brown. (For hard rolls, bake in 400° F oven for 10 minutes, brush with additional egg mixture if desired, and bake 15 minutes longer.) Cool on wire racks.

11. To store: Seal in plastic bags.

Makes 1 long loaf or 16 hard rolls.

NUTRITIONAL ANALYSIS FOR MENU:
Anniversary Dinner For Two
Analysis based on 1 serving of each recipe listed in menu. For individual recipe analysis, see Appendix.

	Nondairy Option	Dairy Option
Calories	582 kcal.	498 kcal.
Protein	25.92 g.; 59% USRDA	23.82 g.; 54% USRDA
Carbohydrate	88.69 g.	85.39 g.
Total Fat	18.23 g.	9.887 g.
Polyunsaturated Fat	4.501 g.	1.130 g.
Monounsaturated Fat	8.822 g.	5.287 g.
Saturated Fat	2.513 g.	1.602 g.
Cholesterol	0.000 mg.	2.500 mg.
Sodium	455.6 mg.; 21% USRDA	688.6 mg.; 31% USRDA
Iron	13.17 mg.; 73% USRDA	6.636 mg.; 37% USRDA
Calcium	330.8 mg.; 41% USRDA	235.8 mg.; 29% USRDA
Fiber	9.720 g.	9.710 g.

Nondairy Option	Dairy Option
Diabetic Exchanges:	Diabetic Exchanges:
Milk: 0.0; Veg.: 4.6; Fruit: 0.0	Milk: 0.0; Veg.: 4.1; Fruit: 0.0
Bread: 3.7; Meat: 1.3; Fat: 2.7	Bread: 3.7; Meat: 1.0; Fat: 1.5

SPECIAL OCCASIONS

▶ Anniversary Dinner for Two
▶ **Stars and Stripes Barbecue**
▶ Tailgate Picnic
▶ Valentine Candlelight Dinner
▶ New Year's Eve Pizza Party
▶ Jingle Bells Buffet

*T*IME for the Fourth, fireworks, family, and feasting? Here are some tasty, up-to-date ideas for a fresher, lighter picnic with all the excitement and sparkle a holiday feast should have. And this menu has one added bonus—you'll love yourself on the fifth of July. So fire up the barbecue as a prelude to the fireworks, and let the season's peak produce make its delicious, nutritious contribution to this colorful summertime meal.

Prepare and marinate the vegetables for the kabobs a day ahead. Then assemble them on wood or metal skewers before barbecuing. Make the macaroni salad ahead also, if you wish, and stuff it into tomato cups 1-2 hours before serving time.

The eye-appealing Stars and Stripes Watermelon, filled with fresh fruit, is the perfect centerpiece for a festive picnic table.

◀ **Whether it's a family barbecue by the lake or a picnic eaten on the village green to the accompaniment of a band concert, people all over the world celebrate with food, no matter what their nationality.**

BARBECUED VEGETABLE KABOBS

Serves 8

   2 large carrots, cut crosswise into
      ½-inch slices
  12 small thin-skinned potatoes (2
      inches in diameter)
   3 medium-sized zucchini, cut cross-
      wise into 1-inch slices
   1 red bell pepper, seeded and cut
      into 1-inch squares
   1 green bell pepper, seeded and cut
      into 1-inch squares
   1 large onion, cut in wedges and sep-
      arated into layers
  16 whole large mushrooms
      Lemon-Garlic Dressing (see Varia-
      tions section)
      Salt to taste, optional

   1. Cook carrots in 1-inch of boiling water
until crisp-tender (about 6 minutes); drain.
Cook unpeeled potatoes in 1-inch of boiling
water just until tender (about 20 minutes);
drain and cut in half. To microwave: Place
potatoes in covered dish with 3 tablespoons
of water and microwave on high for about 15
minutes. Add carrots and cook an additional
5-8 minutes until crisp-tender.
   2. Place carrots, potatoes, zucchini, peppers, onion, and mushrooms in a plastic bag.
Prepare Lemon-Garlic Dressing (see Variations section for recipe). Pour dressing over
vegetables, seal bag, and place in refrigerater
to marinate for 2 hours or until next day.
   3. Drain vegetables and reserve marinade.
Thread vegetables onto 8 sturdy metal skewers, alternating varieties.
   Barbecue Option: place on a lightly oiled
grill 4-6 inches above a solid bed of low-
glowing coals. Grill, turning often and basting
with reserved marinade, for 10-15 minutes or
until vegetables are tender. Sprinkle lightly
with salt before serving if desired.
   Oven Option: arrange kabobs on a lightly
oiled baking sheet and bake at 450° F for
about 10-15 minutes or until lightly browned,
basting with dressing several times during
baking.

Makes 8 vegetable kabobs.

STARS AND STRIPES WATERMELON

Serves 16-24

   1 watermelon
  16 to 24 cups fresh or canned fruit cut
      into different shapes

Pictured watermelon bowl contains the following:

   6 cups watermelon chunks
   3 cups cantaloupe, balls or chunks
   3 cups honeydew, balls or chunks
   3 cups green or red seedless grapes,
      whole
   3 cups fresh peaches, sliced
   3 cups fresh strawberries, whole
   3 cups fresh or frozen blueberries
      Try additional fruits such as kiwi,
      pineapple, apples, orange sections,
      bananas, etc.
   2 cups orange juice concentrate or 3
      cups Fruit Salad Dressing (see rec-
      ipe following)
      Mint sprigs to garnish, optional

   1. To carve melon bowl, cut off top ⅓ of
melon horizontally. Cut thin slice from bottom of melon so it will stand flat, being careful not to cut through melon. Scoop out watermelon contents, leaving ½-1-inch thick
shell.
   2. With pen or pencil, trace around a 1-2
inch star-shaped cookie cutter held against
the cut edge of watermelon, forming a band
of stars along edge. Cut ¾ of the way around
each star with small sharp knife, forming a
star-shaped border. Wrap melon bowl in foil
to keep moist; refrigerate until ready to
serve. (For a smaller watermelon bowl, cut
melon vertically across center, and use one
of the ends for bowl. Don't forget to cut a flat
spot on end of melon so the bowl will stand.)
   3. Place an assortment of fruit cut in a variety of shapes into watermelon bowl. Drizzle
orange juice concentrate or Fruit Salad
Dressing (recipe following) over top and toss
lightly with fruit. Garnish with sprigs of mint
if desired.

FRUIT SALAD DRESSING
Serves 24

- 1 **cup plain yogurt or tofu, blended with 1 tablespoon oil**
- 2 **tablespooons unsweetened orange juice**
- 2 **tablespoons unsweetened pineapple juice**
- ½ **teaspoon vanilla, optional**
- ½ **cup coconut, optional**

Blend yogurt or tofu and 1 tablespoon oil with orange juice and pineapple juice. Stir in optional ingredients if desired. Chill and serve over fruit salad. Double recipe for Stars and Stripes Watermelon fruit salad.

Makes 1½ cups.

MACARONI SALAD IN TOMATO CUPS
Serves 6-8

- 6-8 **medium tomatoes, chilled**
- 1 **cup uncooked macaroni**
- ⅛ **cup chopped green pepper**
- ⅛ **cup chopped red pepper**
- 1 **medium stalk celery, sliced thinly**
- 1 **to 2 green onions with tops, sliced thinly**
- ½ **cup frozen peas**
- 3 **hard-boiled eggs, discard yolks and chop egg whites (optional)**
- ¾ **to 1 cup nondairy Dilly Delight Dressing (see Variations section) or mayonnaise**
  Garlic powder to taste
  Salt to taste, optional

1. Cook macaroni according to package directions to make 2½ cups cooked pasta. Drain macaroni, and add green and red peppers, celery, green onions, and peas. Add chopped egg whites if desired.
2. Prepare nondairy Dilly Delight Dressing if desired (see recipe in Variations section). Pour dressing or mayonnaise over macaroni and vegetables and toss lightly. Chill.

3. To prepare tomatoes: Cut out stems of 6-8 chilled tomatoes. Carefully cut each tomato into six wedges, cutting to within ½ inch of bottom. Spread out sections, forming a cup. Sprinkle inside of each tomato with salt, if desired. Place about ½ cup of macaroni salad into each tomato cup. Serve chilled on a lettuce leaf.

Makes 6-8 tomato cups.

ROASTED CORN ON THE COB
Serves 8

- 8 **to 12 ears of sweet corn with husks**
  Margarine to taste, optional
  Salt to taste, optional

Remove large outer husks from ears; turn back inner husks and remove silk. Spread corn with margarine, if desired. Pull inner husks back over ears and wrap each ear securely in heavy-duty aluminum foil, twisting ends to make handles for turning. Roast corn directly on medium coals 10-15 minutes, turning once. Or grill 3 inches from hot coals 20-30 minutes, turning frequently. Serve hot with salt to taste, if desired.

Makes 8-12 ears of corn.

HOT HERBED GARLIC BREAD
Serves 16-24

- 1 **loaf homemade Whole-Wheat Italian Bread (recipe in Anniversary Dinner for Two menu) or 1 loaf purchased Italian bread**
- 6 **tablespoons olive oil**
- 6 **teaspoons freshly grated Parmesan cheese or Nondairy Parmesan Cheese (see Variations section)**
- 6 **teaspoons fresh chopped basil leaves, or 2-3 teaspoons dry basil**
- 2 **large garlic cloves, peeled and minced, or 2-3 teaspoons garlic powder or to taste**
  Salt to taste, optional

1. In a small bowl, mix Parmesan cheese, basil, and garlic. Add salt to taste if desired.
2. Slice bread loaf into ½-inch slices. Brush olive oil on each slice. Spread cheese-and-basil mixture on bread.
3. Reassemble loaf and wrap in heavy-duty aluminum foil; seal securely. Heat on grill 4 inches from medium coals 15 to 20 minutes, turning once. Or arrange slices with oil and cheese toppings on baking sheet and place under broiler for 2 to 3 minutes, until bread is lightly browned, crisp and bubbly. Serve hot.

Makes 16-24 slices.

MINTED ICY LEMONADE
Serves 8

**12 ounces frozen lemonade concentrate, rediluted according to directions on can
Fresh mint leaves**

1. Prepare lemonade.
2. Lightly bruise 12-15 mint leaves between fingers to release aroma. Place mint leaves in glasses filled with ice. Pour lemonade in glasses and garnish with one mint sprig per glass.

Makes 2 quarts.

NUTRITIONAL ANALYSIS FOR MENU:
Stars and Stripes Barbecue
Analysis based on 1 serving of each recipe listed in menu.
For individual recipe analysis, see Appendix.

	Nondairy Option	Dairy Option
Calories	701 kcal.	795 kcal.
Protein	18.57 g.; 42% USRDA	14.94 g.; 34% USRDA
Carbohydrate	132.4 g.	131.7 g.
Total Fat	16.43 g.	28.43 g.
Polyunsaturated Fat	3.321 g.	10.14 g.
Monounsaturated Fat	9.154 g.	11.75 g.
Saturated Fat	2.350 g.	4.308 g.
Cholesterol	0.000 mg.	13.16 mg.
Sodium	275.9 mg.; 13% USRDA	339.7 mg.; 15% USRDA
Iron	7.530 mg.; 42% USRDA	4.412 mg.; 25% USRDA
Calcium	145.8 mg.; 18% USRDA	116.0 mg.; 15% USRDA
Fiber	17.55 g.	17.46 g.

Nondairy Option
Diabetic Exchanges:
Milk: 0.0; Veg.: 2.3; Fruit: 3.0
Bread: 4.7; Meat: 0.6; Fat: 2.6

Dairy Option
Diabetic Exchanges:
Milk: 0.1; Veg.: 2.1; Fruit: 3.0
Bread: 4.7; Meat: 0.1; Fat: 5.6

SPECIAL OCCASIONS

▶ Anniversary Dinner for Two
▶ Stars and Stripes Barbecue
▶ **Tailgate Picnic**
▶ Valentine Candlelight Dinner
▶ New Year's Eve Pizza Party
▶ Jingle Bells Buffet

*P*ICKUP *trucks and station wagons. Fresh, crisp fall air. Banter between friendly rivals. It's the season for football games and tailgate picnics. When you lay out this casual but festive picnic lunch to begin the pregame fanfare, you'll be a winner, no matter what happens on the field.*

Make the pita bread ahead (follow the recipe in the Greek Luncheon, p. 36), or buy ready-made pita rounds. (It's a good idea to keep a supply of pita bread in the freezer for spontaneous picnics and parties.) The Carob-coated Bonbons make a great finger-food dessert that can be made ahead and frozen. (The recipe is in the dessert menu.)

Just before packing the car, arrange the vegetables on a bed of ice in a bowl or basket. Cut the pita pizzas into wedges, arrange them on a platter and wrap in foil to keep them warm. Pack up the chips, dip, and bonbons, and you're on your way to a great afternoon of friends, healthy food, and football. Go, team!

◀ **Who could resist this delightful picnic setting, with its baskets of healthful and delicious treats?**

PITA BREAD PIZZAS

Serves 4-6

- ¼ **cup chopped onion**
- ¼ **cup chopped green pepper, optional**
- ½ **cup sliced fresh mushrooms**
- ¼ **teaspoon basil**
- ¼ **teaspoon oregano**
- ¼ **teaspoon garlic powder**
- ¼ **cup sliced black olives**
- ⅛ **cup chopped green chilies**
- 1 **cup canned or homemade tomato sauce (see recipe in Italian at Its Best menu)**
- 1 **cup finely grated mozzarella cheese or ¾ cup Nondairy Pimento Cheese (see Variations section)**
- 3 **tablespoons olive oil, optional**
- 8 **to 10 6-inch pita bread rounds, purchased or homemade (see recipe in Greek Luncheon menu)**

1. If making homemade pita bread and/or homemade tomato sauce, prepare ahead, following directions with recipe.

2. In a large skillet over medium-high heat, sauté onion in small amount of water or oil. (If using water, cover skillet during cooking.) Add green peppers and cook until tender. Add mushrooms, basil, oregano, and garlic powder, and sauté for 1 minute, stirring frequently. Remove from heat and let cool slightly.

3. Stir in black olives, chopped green chilies, tomato sauce, and grated mozzarella cheese or nondairy cheese.

4. Place pita rounds on a baking sheet. Brush top of each round with small amount of olive oil if desired. Spread tomato-vegetable mixture evenly over pita rounds. (Pita pizzas freeze well at this point.)

5. Bake in preheated 425° F oven for 5-10 minutes or until cheese is bubbly. (If using nondairy cheese, mixture will require more baking time to get bubbly.)

6. Serve whole pita pizzas hot. Or cut each round into 4-6 wedges and arrange on serving plate.

Makes 8-10 pita pizzas.

GARDEN FRESH BASKET OF VEGETABLES

Serves 4-6

- 2 **cups fresh broccoli spears**
- 2 **cups fresh cauliflower flowerets**
- 8 **carrots, cut in 4- to 6-inch julienne sticks**
- 1 **green pepper, cut in thick slices**
- 8 **celery stalks, cut into 4- to 6-inch sticks with some leaves reserved for garnishing**
- 6 **to 8 green onions, whole**
- 10 **cherry tomatoes, whole with stems**
- 3 **to 4 lettuce leaves**

1. Wash and prepare vegetables, or any other fresh raw vegetables you choose. Place vegetables in sealed plastic bags and refrigerate until serving time.

2. Fill a large serving bowl about half full of crushed ice. Cover ice with plastic wrap, then cover plastic wrap with lettuce leaves. Just before serving, arrange vegetables on lettuce leaves. (You may need to drain water as the ice melts.) Place serving bowl with arranged vegetables inside a basket to serve if desired.

TOASTED CORN TORTILLA CHIPS

Serves 4 (12 chips per serving)

(See recipe in La Fiesta Grande menu)

HOT ARTICHOKE DIP

Serves 16-32

- 3 **4-ounce cans artichoke hearts, drained**
- ¾ **cup low-fat mayonnaise or Nondairy Tofu Sour Cream (see Variations section)**
- ¾ **cup freshly grated parmesan cheese, or ½ cup canned grated Parmesan cheese, or ½ cup Nondairy Parmesan Cheese (see Variations section for recipe)**
- **Paprika to garnish**

1. Place artichoke hearts, mayonnaise, and Parmesan cheese in food processor or blender and process until smooth or slightly chunky, depending on how you like it.

2. Place mixture in oven-safe serving bowl. Top with paprika. Bake at 350° F for 20 to 30 minutes or until lightly browned and bubbly.

Note: Nutrition analysis for menu is based on 1 tablespoon per serving.

Makes approximately 2 cups or 32 1-tablespoon servings or 16 2-tablespoon servings.

NUTRITIONAL ANALYSIS FOR MENU:
Tailgate Picnic

Analysis based on 1 serving of each recipe listed in menu. For individual recipe analysis, see Appendix.

	Nondairy Option	Dairy Option
Calories	448 kcal.	557 kcal.
Protein	17.47 g.; 40% USRDA	29.51 g.; 67% USRDA
Carbohydrate	84.45 g.	81.13 g.
Total Fat	8.557 g.	16.27 g.
Polyunsaturated Fat	1.750 g.	0.759 g.
Monounsaturated Fat	2.078 g.	3.639 g.
Saturated Fat	0.872 g.	6.498 g.
Cholesterol	0.000 mg.	35.51 mg.
Sodium	633.4 mg.; 29% USRDA	839.3 mg.; 38% USRDA
Iron	7.195 mg.; 40% USRDA	5.822 mg.; 32% USRDA
Calcium	257.5 mg.; 32% USRDA	617.8 mg.; 77% USRDA
Fiber	16.42 g.	15.23 g.

Nondairy Option
Diabetic Exchanges:
Milk: 0.0; Veg.: 4.7; Fruit: 0.2
Bread: 3.4; Meat: 0.3; Fat: 1.4

Dairy Option
Diabetic Exchanges:
Milk: 0.0; Veg.: 4.7; Fruit: 0.1
Bread: 3.3; Meat: 2.1; Fat: 2.2

SPECIAL OCCASIONS

▶ Anniversary Dinner for Two
▶ Stars and Stripes Barbecue
▶ Tailgate Picnic
▶ **Valentine Candlelight Dinner**
▶ New Year's Eve Pizza Party
▶ Jingle Bells Buffet

*F*RENCH CUISINE—it conjures up notions of soft lights, small romantic cafés, and very special dinners for two. It also makes most people think of rich, buttery sauces and lavish desserts. But elegant, special-occasion French cooking doesn't have to be loaded with calories and fat. You can develop your own version of French "nouvelle cuisine"—light and delicious, and beautiful to look at, too.

Make this special French dinner for the very special person in your life. You'll show how much you care, not only with exquisite flavors and a beautifully presented meal, but also with your concern for the good health of the one you love.

The crepes in this menu have been lightened by using nonfat milk or Cashew-Rice Milk in place of cream. Low-fat mozzarella cheese or tofu replace high-fat cheeses. Choose either the dairy or the nondairy options. Both are delicious.

Try the French Apple Tart recipe, in the dessert menu, for a grand finale to this special meal. This dessert adds light, refreshing apple and apricot flavors that provide the perfect finish.

◀ *The mood is romantic, the food is French, the dishes are family heirlooms, and the setting is pure storybook. To accompany this special dinner, choose a pretty pink beverage.*

GARDEN VEGETABLE CREPES

Serves 6-8

  10 **French Crepes or Cholesterol Free Oat crepes (see recipes in the Bridal Shower Brunch Menu, pp. 29 and 30)**

1½ **cups Béchamel Sauce (see recipe following)**

   1 **cup Broccoli or Spinach Filling (see recipe following)**

 ¾ **cup Mushroom Filling (see recipe following)**

   3 **tablespoons freshly grated Parmesan cheese, or Nondairy Parmesan Cheese (see Variations section)**

 ¼ **cup sliced almonds, optional**
     Paprika to garnish

1. Prepare French or low-cholesterol oat crepes, according to your preference. Then make the Béchamel Sauce, Broccoli or Spinach Filling, and Mushroom Filling according to recipes following.

2. Preheat oven to 350° F. Lightly oil a 9-inch round baking dish.

3. Place a crepe in the bottom of the baking dish. Spread on it a thin layer of Mushroom Filling (about 2 tablespoons). Top with a crepe and spread on a layer of Broccoli or Spinach Filling. Continue alternating layers of crepes and fillings for 9 layers. End with a crepe.

4. Pour the Béchamel Sauce over the top and sides of crepe stack, and sprinkle with Parmesan cheese. Bake to heat through and lightly brown the top, about 20-25 minutes. Garnish with almond slices and paprika if desired. To serve, cut into wedges. (To prepare this recipe ahead of time, make the crepes, fillings, and sauce; refrigerate separately. Assemble and bake the crepe stack just before serving.)

Note: Menu nutrition analysis is based on 6 servings per recipe.

BÉCHAMEL SAUCE

Serves 8

1½ **tablespoons margarine**

1½ **tablespoons flour**

1⅛ **cups skim milk, soy milk, tofu milk, or Cashew-Rice Milk (see Variations section)**
     Salt to taste, optional

 ½ **teaspoon basil**

 ½ **teaspoon garlic powder**

 ½ **teaspoon onion powder**

 ½ **cup finely grated mozzarella cheese, optional**

In a saucepan, melt the margarine; add the flour and stir over medium heat until bubbly. Remove from heat and stir in the milk. Return to heat and cook, stirring constantly, until the sauce is smooth and thick. Stir in seasonings. Add cheese if desired. Continue stirring over low heat until the cheese has melted. Set aside.

Makes 1½ cups.

BROCCOLI OR SPINACH FILLING

Serves 8

   1 **tablespoon margarine or 2 tablespoons water**

   2 **scallions or green onions, minced**

 ½ **cup cooked and finely chopped broccoli or ½ cup cooked and finely chopped spinach**

 ¼ **cup sliced almonds**
     Salt to taste, optional

 ½ **cup Cottage Cheese Sauce (see recipe following) or Nondairy Tofu Cheese Sauce (see recipe following)**

1. In a small saucepan, sauté the scallions or green onions in margarine or water until softened. (If sautéing in water, cover skillet during cooking.)

2. Add broccoli or spinach, with moisture removed from spinach, to onions. Stir in almonds. Add salt to taste, if desired. Cook, stirring constantly, over medium-high heat for about 3 minutes. Remove from heat; stir in the Cottage Cheese Sauce or Nondairy Tofu Cheese Sauce. Set aside.

Makes about 1 cup.

MUSHROOM FILLING
Serves 8

   2 tablespoons margarine or water
   8 ounces mushrooms, chopped
   2 scallions or green onions, minced
      Salt to taste, optional
   ½ cup Cottage Cheese Sauce (see recipe following) or Nondairy Tofu Cheese Sauce (see recipe following)

1. In a small skillet, sauté the mushrooms and scallions or green onions in margarine or water until softened. (If using water, cover pan during cooking.) Drain if necessary and add salt to taste, if desired.
2. Stir in Cottage Cheese Sauce or Nondairy Tofu Cheese Sauce. Set aside.

Makes ¾ cup.

COTTAGE CHEESE SAUCE
Serves 8

   1 cup low-fat cottage cheese
   2 egg whites
   ½ teaspoon garlic powder
   ½ teaspoon dried basil

In a food processor or blender, puree the cottage cheese and egg whites until smooth. Add to vegetable fillings.

Makes 1 cup.

NONDAIRY TOFU CHEESE SAUCE
Serves 8

   1 cup tofu
   ½ teaspoon garlic powder
   ½ teaspoon dried basil
   ¼ teaspoon lemon juice
   ½ teaspoon honey

Puree all ingredients in food processor or blender. Add to vegetable fillings.

Makes 1 cup.

TOMATO AND MUSHROOM MARINATED SALAD
Serves 6-8

   4 medium tomatoes, peeled and cut into thick slices
   30 small whole mushrooms
Dressing
   ½ cup olive oil or other vegetable oil or ¼ cup oil and ¼ cup water
   ¼ cup lemon juice
   ¼ cup finely chopped fresh parsley or 2 tablespoons dried parsley
   ¼ cup finely chopped green onions with tops
   1 garlic clove, minced
   1 teaspoon salt or to taste, optional
   1 teaspoon dill weed
   1 teaspoon basil leaves
      Fresh spinach leaves or green leafy lettuce leaves

1. Place tomatoes and mushrooms in serving dish. To make dressing, combine the remaining ingredients in small bowl or screw-top jar and mix well.
2. Pour dressing over tomatoes and mushrooms. Cover; refrigerate 1-2 hours, basting occasionally.
3. On individual serving dishes, arrange spinach or lettuce leaves. Place marinated

tomatoes and mushrooms on leaves, and pour small amount of marinated dressing over vegetables if desired.

Note: Nutrition analysis is based on draining off ¼ cup of oil and water marinade.

WHOLE-WHEAT CRESCENT ROLLS

Serves 12-24

- 1½ **cups whole-wheat flour**
- 1½ **cups all-purpose flour**
- ¼ **cup wheat germ**
- 1 **package active dry yeast**
- ½ **cup warm water (about 110° F)**
- 1½ **tablespoons honey**
- 1½ **teaspoons salt**
- ½ **cup warm water (about 110° F)**
- 2½ **tablespoons melted margarine**
- 2 **egg whites, slightly beaten, or ⅓ cup tofu, blended smooth**
- 1½ **teaspoons melted margarine, optional**
- 1 **egg white, beaten, optional**

1. In a bowl, mix together whole wheat flour, all-purpose flour, and wheat germ.

2. In a separate large bowl, dissolve yeast in ½ cup warm water. Add honey, salt, additional ½ cup warm water, melted margarine, and egg whites or tofu. Beat in 1½ cups of the flour mixture, ½ cup at a time, and then beat until dough is elastic (about 5 minutes at medium speed if using electric mixer).

3. With a heavy-duty mixer or wooden spoon, gradually beat in remaining flour mixture. Dough should be soft, but not too sticky to knead. If necessary, add additional all-purpose flour to prevent sticking. Turn dough out onto a floured board and knead just until smooth. Let rest 10 minutes.

4. Divide dough into 2 equal parts; shape each into a smooth ball. On a floured board, using a lightly floured rolling pin, roll out each ball into a 12-inch circle. Brush with melted margarine (if desired), and cut into 12 equal wedges. Starting from the wide end, use your hands to roll up each wedge toward point. Place rolls, points down, 2 inches apart on well-oiled baking sheets. Curve each roll slightly. Brush lightly with 1 egg white,

beaten with 1 tablespoon water, if desired. (This step gives crescent rolls a shiny, golden-brown, crispy appearance.)

5. Cover with a towel and let rise in warm place until very puffy (about 45 minutes). Bake in a preheated 400° F oven for about 15 minutes or until golden. Remove from pan and cool on wire racks.

6. To store: Place cooled rolls in plastic bags and seal tightly to preserve freshness.

7. To warm rolls: Place in paper bag, sprinkle bag with water, fold down top, and heat in 325° F oven for 10 minutes or until heated thoroughly. To warm in microwave: Place in bag as above and heat at medium-high heat for about 30 seconds for 4 rolls. Microwave for less time for less rolls and more time for more rolls. These rolls freeze well.

Note: Menu nutrition analysis is based on 2 rolls per serving.

Makes 24 crescent rolls.

NUTRITIONAL ANALYSIS FOR MENU:
Valentine Candlelight Dinner
Analysis based on 1 serving of each recipe listed in menu.
For individual recipe analysis, see Appendix.

	Nondairy Option	Dairy Option
Calories	407 kcal.	451 kcal.
Protein	17.84 g.; 41% USRDA	26.06 g.; 59% USRDA
Carbohydrate	47.17 g.	57.67 g.
Total Fat	18.95 g.	14.73 g.
Polyunsaturated Fat	4.670 g.	3.749 g.
Monounsaturated Fat	8.954 g.	6.619 g.
Saturated Fat	2.760 g.	2.918 g.
Cholesterol	0.000 mg.	6.330 mg.
Sodium	163.9 mg.; 7% USRDA	533.9 mg.; 24% USRDA
Iron	8.564 mg.; 48% USRDA	5.491 mg.; 31% USRDA
Calcium	165.4 mg.; 21% USRDA	334.9 mg.; 42% USRDA
Fiber	7.500 g.	9.235 g.

Nondairy Option
Diabetic Exchanges:
Milk: 0.1; Veg.: 2.0; Fruit: 0.0
Bread: 2.1; Meat: 0.8; Fat: 3.4

Dairy Option
Diabetic Exchanges:
Milk: 0.5; Veg.: 1.7; Fruit: 0.0
Bread: 2.6; Meat: 1.4; Fat: 2.478

SPECIAL OCCASIONS

▶ Anniversary Dinner for Two
▶ Stars and Stripes Barbecue
▶ Tailgate Picnic
▶ Valentine Candlelight Dinner
▶ **New Year's Eve Pizza Party**
▶ Jingle Bells Buffet

*P*IZZA AND popcorn—ingredients for impromptu entertaining at its best. Whether it's New Year's Eve or just a Saturday night get-together, the menu couldn't be simpler—or more delicious. Choose these gourmet pizza versions when you want to do something easy but just a little bit special. And what better occasion to introduce heart-healthy, low-cholesterol versions of old favorites than New Year's Eve, the perfect time for making resolutions about eating smarter?

Fresh vegetables in colorful sweet pepper cups, served with a delicious, nondairy, creamy dill dressing, start this party meal in spectacular fashion. The toppings for the Vegetarian Supreme Pizza are sure to please the most refined gourmet. Both pizza recipes use low-fat mozzarella cheese or Nondairy Pimento Cheese.

Top off the meal with Strawberry Tofu Ice Cream. This great dessert (found in the dessert menu) can be made without dairy products, thus eliminating cholesterol with no sacrifice in taste—great news for you ice-cream lovers.

◀ *Paper plates and napkins, confetti and noisemakers—the scene is set for an evening of good food and fun.*

VEGETARIAN SUPREME PIZZA

Serves 8-10

- 1 **14-inch Whole-Wheat Pizza Dough (recipe following)**
- 2 **cups Pizza Sauce (recipe following)**
- 2 **cups grated mozzarella cheese or Nondairy Pimento Cheese (see Variations section)**
- 4 **small zucchini, sliced thinly**
- 2 **cups fresh or well-drained frozen spinach**
- 4 **green onions with tops, sliced, or 1 medium onion, chopped**
- 2 **garlic cloves, minced**
- 1 **green or red pepper, sliced lengthwise**
- 1 **teaspoon dried basil**
- ½ **teaspoon oregano**
- ½ **cup sliced mushrooms**
- ½ **cup sliced black olives, optional**
- 1 **can artichoke hearts, drained and quartered, optional**
- 2 **medium tomatoes, thinly sliced**
- 1½ **to 2 cups sliced almonds, optional Olive oil, optional**

1. Prepare Pizza Dough and Pizza Sauce with following recipes.
2. Steam spinach, zucchini, onion, garlic, and peppers in covered skillet with small amount of water, until crisp-tender. Stir in basil and oregano.
3. Spread crust with 1 teaspoon olive oil, if desired. Spread crust with pizza sauce; top with cheese. Arrange sautéed vegetable mixture over cheese. Add mushrooms, black olives, and artichokes in layers. Sprinkle additional cheese on top if desired.
4. Fold in overhanging crust to form border around filling. Press border at 1-inch intervals to seal. Bake on lowest oven rack 10 minutes at 525° F; reduce heat to 450° F and bake 10 to 12 minutes or until crust is lightly browned.
5. Arrange fresh tomatoes on top of pizza, and sprinkle top with almonds if desired. Serve at once.

Makes 1 14-inch pizza.

WHOLE-WHEAT PIZZA DOUGH

Serves 16

- 1 **package active dry yeast**
- 1 **cup warm water (110° F)**
- 1 **teaspoon honey**
- 1 **teaspoon salt**
- 2 **tablespoon olive oil or other vegetable oil**
- 2½ **cups whole-wheat flour Cornmeal**

1. In medium-sized bowl, dissolve yeast in warm water with honey. Stir in remaining ingredients; beat vigorously 20 strokes. Be sure all flour is absorbed. Form into ball and let rest 5 minutes.
2. Lightly oil bottom of 14-inch pizza pan; sprinkle with cornmeal.
3. Divide dough in half. (This recipe makes enough for 2 crusts. If you're making only one pizza, freeze extra crust after rolling out.) With lightly floured rolling pin, roll dough on very lightly floured surface into 15-inch circle. Place dough over pizza pan and press down to fit, leaving edges overlapping about 1 inch. Continue with pizza recipe for toppings and baking instructions.

Makes 2 14-inch pizza crusts.

PIZZA SAUCE

Serves 8

- 2 **cloves garlic, finely minced**
- 1 **tablespoon olive oil or 1 tablespoon water**
- 1½ **cups canned Italian-style plum tomatoes, drained and chopped**
- ¼ **cup tomato paste**
- 1½ **teaspoons dried crushed oregano leaves**
- ½ **teaspoon basil**
- ¼ **teaspoon salt, optional**
- ¼ **teaspoon lemon juice, optional Dash of sugar, optional**

1. Sauté minced garlic in oil or water in medium-sized saucepan over medium heat 20 seconds. Add chopped tomatoes, tomato

paste, oregano, and basil. Add salt, lemon juice, and sugar, if desired. Sauté 5 minutes; reduce heat to low. Cook uncovered, stirring occasionally, for 10 minutes. Remove from heat. Sauce is ready to use.

2. Continue with directions for pizza.

Makes about 2 cups.

FRESH TOMATOES AND CHEESE PIZZA
Serves 8

 1 **14-inch Whole-Wheat Pizza Dough (see recipe with Vegetarian Supreme Pizza)**
 2 **cups Pizza Sauce (recipe with Vegetarian Supreme Pizza)**
 3 **cups grated mozzarella cheese or 2 cups Nondairy Pimento Cheese (see Variations section)**
 3 **to 4 medium-sized tomatoes, sliced**

1. Prepare Pizza Dough and Pizza Sauce according to directions.

2. Spread crust with 1 teaspoon of olive oil, if desired. Spread with tomato mixture; top with the cheese.

3. Fold in overhanging crust edge to form border around filling. Press border at 1-inch intervals to seal. Bake in preheated 525° F oven on lowest rack for 10 minutes; reduce heat to 450° F and bake 10-12 minutes longer, or until cheese melts and crust begins to brown. Remove from oven.

4. Arrange fresh tomato slices in a circular pattern on top of cheese. Serve immediately.

Makes 1 14-inch pizza.

ANTIPASTO VEGGIE CUPS
Serves 8

 4 **medium-sized sweet red, green, or yellow peppers**
 3 **carrots, quartered and cut into 3-inch strips**
 2 **cucumbers, cut into 3-inch strips or sliced**
 8 **cherry tomatoes**
 8 **radish roses**
16 **green-onion fans**
 8 **whole raw jalapeño peppers, optional**
    Dilly Delight Dip (see Variations section)

1. Choose assorted colors of peppers of the same approximate size and shape that stand upright. Cut a thin slice from the top of each pepper, remove seeds. Cut a thin slice from the bottom of each pepper, if necessary, to help pepper stand upright.

2. Wash and prepare the remaining vegetables. Arrange equal amounts of carrots, cucumbers, cherry tomatoes, radishes, green-onion fans, and jalapeño peppers (if desired) in each pepper cup. Chill thoroughly.

3. Prepare Dilly Delight Dip (see Variations section) or vegetable dip of choice and place in pepper cup or serving dish.

4. Vary this recipe by choosing other vegetables besides peppers as vegetable cups for dip. A hollowed artichoke, green or red cabbage, eggplant, etc., all work as well.

Note: Nutrition analysis for menu based on 1 tablespoon per serving.

SPECIALLY SEASONED POPCORN
Serves 8

½ **cup unpopped popcorn**
 3 **tablespoons margarine, melted, optional**
1½ **to 2 tablespoons or to taste yellow imitation yeast flakes (see How to Get Started section).**
    Salt to taste, optional

1. Pop corn in a hot-air popper and place in a large bowl. (Any other method of popping may also be used, but nutrition information does not include any oil used in popping.)

2. Drizzle melted margarine over popcorn (if desired), tossing or stirring to coat popcorn evenly. (If you choose not to use margarine, try lightly spraying popcorn with soft mist of water to help the yeast flakes and optional salt to stick.)

3. Sprinkle with yeast flakes. Serve warm.
4. To store: Place leftover popcorn in sealed plastic bags.

Makes about 8-12 cups.

NUTRITIONAL ANALYSIS FOR MENU:
New Year's Eve Pizza Party
Analysis based on 1 serving of each recipe listed in menu.
For individual recipe analysis, see Appendix.

	Nondairy Option	Dairy Option
Calories	492 kcal.	564 kcal.
Protein	20.62 g.; 47% USRDA	33.83 g.; 77% USRDA
Carbohydrate	83.56 g.	71.66 g.
Total Fat	12.84 g.	19.47 g.
Polyunsaturated Fat	2.364 g.	2.073 g.
Monounsaturated Fat	5.980 g.	7.110 g.
Saturated Fat	1.932 g.	8.411 g.
Cholesterol	0.000 mg.	40.00 mg.
Sodium	905.2 mg.; 41% USRDA	999.0 mg.; 44% USRDA
Iron	10.90 mg.; 53% USRDA	8.893 mg.; 49% USRDA
Calcium	237.0 mg.; 30% USRDA	664.3 mg.; 83% USRDA
Fiber	16.82 g.	13.44 g.

Nondairy Option	Dairy Option
Diabetic Exchanges:	Diabetic Exchanges:
Milk: 0.0; Veg.: 5.8; Fruit: 0.1	Milk: 0.0; Veg.: 5.6; Fruit: 0.0
Bread: 3.0; Meat: 0.9; Fat: 1.9	Bread: 2.3; Meat: 2.6; Fat: 2.6

SPECIAL OCCASIONS

▶ Anniversary Dinner for Two
▶ Stars and Stripes Barbecue
▶ Tailgate Picnic
▶ Valentine Candlelight Dinner
▶ New Year's Eve Pizza Party
▶ **Jingle Bells Buffet**

*O*UTSIDE the old stone farmhouse the air is crisp and cold, and a light snow is falling. But inside all is warm, bright, and cheery. The rooms are decorated with greenery from the farm's own trees, along with festive red bows and treasured family toys and ornaments. The old house basks in the glow of the fires in each fireplace, and in every window, a candle gleams.

What a perfect time to invite dear friends and family for a delicious open-house Christmas buffet. Here's a tableful of beautiful holiday hors d'oeuvres in the spirit of the season—with the added attraction that everything is good for you!

Use the festive Christmas Fruit Tree as the centerpiece. Make plenty of the Christmas Cooler Punch, and then relax and enjoy your friends and their compliments. Wait a minute. Did you forget the mistletoe?

◀ *An antique sleigh from Vermont serves as the table for this holiday feast. It's Christmas Eve, and the entire room is lavishly decorated for the holiday season with pine boughs, holly, and shiny, dark-green magnolia leaves.*

ARTICHOKE NIBBLES
Serves 25

1 7½-ounce jar marinated artichoke hearts, diced, or plain artichoke hearts, using 3-4 tablespoon Lemon-Garlic Dressing (recipe in Variations section) to sauté onion and garlic
½ cup finely chopped onion
2 garlic cloves, finely chopped, or ½ teaspoon garlic powder
4 egg whites or ½ cup tofu, blended smooth
⅛ cup fine bread crumbs
⅛ teaspoon oregano
⅛ teaspoon salt or to taste, optional
1 cup grated Monterey Jack cheese or Nondairy Pimento Cheese (see Variations section)
1 tablespoon fresh parsley, minced, or 1 teaspoon dried parsley

1. Drain liquid from 1 jar of marinated artichokes into frying pan. In this liquid, sauté onion and garlic until onion is limp, about 5 minutes. (If using plain artichoke hearts, use 3-4 tablespoons garlic dressing (see Variations section) for sautéing onion and garlic.)
2. In separate bowl, beat eggs, or blend tofu in blender until smooth. Add bread crumbs and oregano to eggs or tofu. Add salt to taste, if desired.
3. Add cheese, parsley, diced artichokes, onion, and garlic to egg-and-bread-crumb mixture and stir well to mix. Pour into small (about 5″ x 7″) baking dish and bake at 325° F for 20-25 minutes or until lightly browned. Let cool and cut into 1-inch squares.

Makes about 25 1-inch squares.

FRENCH MUSHROOM TARTS
Serves 18

36 pastry tarts (see recipe following)
¾ cup chopped onion
2 garlic cloves, minced
1 tablespoon margarine or water
1½ cups chopped mushrooms or 1½ cups chopped spinach
½ teaspoon basil, optional
2 eggs, beaten, or 4 egg whites, slightly beaten
3¼ cups sour cream
Option: Replace eggs and sour cream with 3¾ cups Nondairy Tofu Sour Cream (see Variations section for recipe)
1 tablespoon freshly chopped fresh parsley or 1 teaspoon dried parsley
Sliced almonds to garnish, optional

1. Prepare pastry tarts (recipe following).
2. Sauté onion and garlic in margarine or water until tender. (If using water, cover pan during cooking.) Add mushrooms or spinach and basil to sautéed mixture.
3. Place 1 tablespoon of mixture in each tart shell.
4. Mix eggs and sour cream (or Nondairy Tofu Sour Cream) with parsley. Pour over mushroom or spinach filling in tarts until tart is full. Garnish with sliced almonds, if desired.
5. Bake at 350° F for 20 minutes. Serve warm or cool.

Makes 36 small tarts.

TART PASTRY
Serves 18

8 tablespoons margarine
1 cup all-purpose flour or whole-wheat pastry flour
Dash of salt
2 egg whites or ¼ cup tofu, blended smooth
2 tablespoons skim milk, soy milk, or water

1. By hand: Cut margarine into flour until crumbly. Add remaining ingredients, tossing lightly to mix. Form into ball. With food processor: Process all above ingredients together 20-30 seconds or until a ball forms on the side of bowl.

2. With a lightly floured rolling pin, roll pastry out on lightly floured surface and cut into circles 1 inch larger than small tart tins. Form pastry circles into tart tins. (May also use muffin tins for a slightly larger tart.)

Makes about 36 small tart shells.

ZUCCHINI BITES
Serves 9

- **4 small unpeeled zucchini, cut into 1-inch slices**
- **1 tablespoon oil or 1 tablespoon water**
- **⅓ cup chopped tomato**
- **⅓ cup fresh chopped mushrooms**
- **⅓ cup chopped green or red pepper**
- **2 tablespoons minced black olives**
- **⅓ cup finely chopped or grated onion**
- **2 garlic cloves, minced, or 1 teaspoon garlic powder**
- **1 tablespoon fresh chopped basil or 1½ teaspoons dried basil**
- **2 teaspoons fresh chopped oregano or 1 teaspoon dried oregano**
- **½ teaspoon thyme**
  Salt to taste, optional
  Parmesan cheese or Nondairy Parmesan Cheese (see Variations section for recipe) to garnish, optional

1. Cook zucchini slices in steamer basket over boiling water for 3 minutes. Cool slightly and drain well.

2. Working carefully, scoop some of the pulp out of each slice, forming a small cup to hold filling. Be sure to leave small amount of pulp in bottom. Set aside.

3. In large skillet, heat oil or water over medium heat. Add remaining ingredients except cheese and sauté 3 minutes. Drain well.

4. Fill zucchini cups with hot vegetable mixture. Sprinkle with Parmesan cheese or Nondairy Parmesan Cheese, if desired. Serve warm or at room temperature.

Makes 18 zucchini bites.

FRESH VEGETABLE PLATTER
Serves 8-10

- **4 cucumbers, sliced**
- **6 carrots, cut into sticks or curls**
- **3 cups fresh broccoli flowerets**
- **3 cups fresh cauliflower flowerets**
- **6 green onions, whole with ends curled**
- **10 asparagus spears**
- **10 radish roses**
- **10 cherry tomatoes**

1. Prepare vegetables as listed above or any fresh vegetables of your choice. Place in plastic bags and refrigerate until serving time.

2. Arrange vegetables attractively on serving platter. Serve with Avocado-Tomato Dip.

AVOCADO-TOMATO DIP
Serves 20-24

- **1 cup mashed avocado**
- **½ tablespoon lemon juice**
- **¼ teaspoon salt, optional**
- **1½ teaspoons grated onion**
- **2 tablespoons fresh chopped tomatoes**
- **⅛ teaspoon light soy sauce, optional**
  Garlic powder to taste, optional

1. Mix all ingredients, and chill.
2. Serve with vegetable platter.

Makes about 1½ cups.

HERB TOASTED PITA CHIPS/TOASTED CORN TORTILLA CHIPS
(See recipe for pita chips in Greek Luncheon menu)
(See recipe for corn tortilla chips in La Fiesta Grande menu)

Note: 1 serving of pita chips is 4 large chips and 1 serving of corn tortilla chips is 8 wedged chips. This is the information used to calculate menu analysis.

CHRISTMAS FRUIT TREE
Serves 18-24

> 4 **red apples**
> 4 **oranges**
> 1 **cantaloupe**
> 1 **honeydew melon**
> 1 **pineapple**
> 4 **bunches of red grapes**
> 4 **bunches of green grapes**
> 5 **bananas**
> 3 **large bunches of green leaf lettuce**
> **Cranberries to garnish, optional**

1. Wash all fruit. (Use fruits as listed, or vary with your own choice of fresh fruits.) Cut apples in pieces and dip in lemon juice to preserve color. Cut oranges in pieces. Peel and cut melon in small wedges. Peel and cut pineapple into chunks.
2. Place an 18- to 20-inch styrofoam cone on a large platter. Starting at the bottom, place fresh, green leaf lettuce over cone, anchoring with wooden toothpicks where necessary.
3. Starting at the bottom, attach fruit on cone with toothpicks.
4. Arrange greenery around bottom of cone and arrange sprigs of greenery in with fruit if desired. Garnish with cranberries strung onto thread and draped around the tree, to make garland.

Makes 1 20-inch fruit tree.

CHRISTMAS COOLER
Serves 16

> 3 **quarts cranberry juice**
> 1 **quart club soda or 1 quart lemonade**
> 1 **orange, cut into thin slices**
> 8 **to 10 whole cinnamon sticks**

1. Chill juice and soda until serving time.

2. Place cranberry juice and club soda or lemonade in punch bowl or serving pitcher. Float orange slices on top with cinnamon sticks standing through the center of each orange circle. If desired, arrange evergreen or flowers around base of punch bowl. Serve.

Makes 1 gallon or 16 8-ounce servings.

CHRISTMAS TREE BRAID
Serves 36

> 3 **cups whole-wheat flour**
> 4½ **teaspoons whole-wheat gluten flour**
> 2 **packages active dry yeast**
> ½ **cup warm water (115-120° F)**
> 4 **tablespoons margarine**
> 4 **tablespoons honey**
> 1 **teaspoon salt**
> 2 **egg whites or ¼ cup tofu, blended smooth**
> **Honey-Nut Filling (optional)**
> 4 **to 6 tablespoons margarine**
> **Cinnamon to taste, or Cinnamon Substitute (see Variations section)**
> ½ **cup chopped nuts**
> 4 **to 6 tablespoons honey or brown sugar**

1. In large mixing bowl, combine 1 cup whole-wheat flour, 4½ teaspoons whole-wheat gluten flour, and yeast.
2. In separate bowl, combine warm water, margarine, honey or brown sugar, and salt. Stir until margarine is almost melted.
3. Add liquid mixture to flour mixture. Stir in blended tofu or egg whites. (Be sure tofu or egg whites are at room temperature.)
4. Beat at low speed with electric mixer for ½ minute, scraping sides of bowl constantly. Beat 3 minutes at high speed. By hand, stir in 2 cups flour, ½ cup at a time, to make a moderately soft dough.
5. Turn dough out onto a lightly floured surface and knead until smooth and elastic (8-10 minutes). Shape into a ball. Place in lightly oiled bowl, turning once to oil top of dough. Cover and let rise in warm place until doubled in size (about 1 hour).
6. Punch dough down; turn out onto lightly floured surface. Divide dough in half. Cover

with a towel and let rest 10 minutes. Then, with a lightly floured rolling pin, roll each portion into a 10″ x 15″ rectangle. If filling is desired, spread each rectangle with 1 table-spoon margarine, and sprinkle with cinnamon and nuts. Sprinkle brown sugar or drizzle honey over the top. (Leave a 1″ x 12″ strip without filling to form center strip of tree.) Cut each rectangle into 1″ x 15″ strips. (Each rectangle makes one tree.)

7. Place the 12-inch strip (the one without the topping) on an oiled baking sheet for the center of the tree. For bottom branch, take a 15-inch strip and fold it in half longways. Twist the dough to form a spiral, pinching ends to seal. Place the strip ½-inch up from the bottom of the tree's center strip. For the next branch, cut a 1″ x 12″ strip, twist to form spiral, pinch ends, and place above the bottom strip. Continue with the folding, twist-ing, and pinching procedure to form remain-ing branches of tree, using strips that are 1″ x 9″, 1″ x 6″, and 1″ x 3″. Fold top stem un-der to form top of tree. Repeat with remain-ing dough for second tree.

8. Cover with a towel and let rise in warm place until doubled in size (45-60 minutes). Bake at 375° F for 12 to 15 minutes. Using two spatulas, remove from sheets carefully, and cool on racks.

9. To serve, place on platter and decorate with ribbon, evergreen, dried fruit, etc.

Makes 2 trees.

NUTRITIONAL ANALYSIS FOR MENU:
Jingle Bells Buffet
Analysis based on 1 serving of each recipe listed in menu.
For individual recipe analysis, see Appendix.

	Nondairy Option	Dairy Option
Calories	691 kcal.	674 kcal.
Protein	20.08 g.; 46% USRDA	18.95 g.; 43% USRDA
Carbohydrate	122.2 g.	119.9 g.
Total Fat	19.74 g.	18.72 g.
Polyunsaturated Fat	6.469 g.	2.091 g.
Monounsaturated Fat	7.054 g.	6.328 g.
Saturated Fat	2.664 g.	4.283 g.
Cholesterol	0.000 mg.	9.220 mg.
Sodium	484.5 mg.; 22% USRDA	444.2 mg.; 20% USRDA
Iron	9.224 mg.; 51% USRDA	5.809 mg.; 32% USRDA
Calcium	275.1 mg.; 34% USRDA	302.4 mg.; 38% USRDA
Fiber	17.07 g.	16.80 g.

Nondairy Option	Dairy Option
Diabetic Exchanges:	Diabetic Exchanges:
Milk: 0.0; Veg.: 4.0; Fruit: 2.4	Milk: 0.0; Veg.: 3.7; Fruit: 4.1
Bread: 2.4; Meat: 0.7; Fat: 3.5	Bread: 2.3; Meat: 0.5; Fat: 3.6

▶ Delightfully Healthy Desserts

*W*HO SAYS diet-conscious people have to skip dessert? Luscious low-calorie low-sugar desserts are possible, even on special diets, when you rely on the flavors and natural goodness of fruit. These glorious finales for healthy meals include a spectacular Rainbow Fruit Terrine, an attractive and tasty Fresh Fruit Platter Pie, an unforgettable French Apple Tart, and a cool, refreshing Pear Sorbet With Raspberry Sauce. Be sure to give the Carob-coated Bonbons a try. With or without the carob coating, they are unbelievably delicious.

◀ *An antique pine corner cupboard provides the backdrop for a fantasy array of delicious and healthy desserts.*

RAINBOW FRUIT TERRINE
Serves 10

   1 **12-ounce package frozen raspberries, partially thawed (or use frozen strawberries)**
   6 **to 8 tablespoons, or to taste, sweetener—honey, sugar, or apple juice concentrate**
   6 **fresh kiwi fruit, peeled**
   2 **medium-sized ripe papayas or 4 large peaches, peeled, halved, and seeded (or 12 ounces frozen peaches)**
   1 **tablespoon lime juice**

   1. Line an 8″ x 4″ loaf pan with aluminum foil.
   2. In blender, puree raspberries with 2-4 tablespoons of desired sweetener. Pour into pan; freeze 1 hour.
   3. Puree kiwi with 2 tablespoons sweetener. Pour over raspberry layer; freeze 1 hour.
   4. Puree papaya or peaches with 2 tablespoons sweetener and the lime juice; pour over kiwi layer. Freeze overnight or until firm.
   5. Unmold terrine onto platter; garnish with additional kiwi slices or fresh fruit of choice, if desired. Refrigerate ½ hour, or until soft enough to slice.
   6. Serve and enjoy the luscious fresh flavor of fruit.

BERRY-MELON COMPOTE
Serves 8

   ½ **cup unsweetened orange juice**
   ⅓ **cup unsweetened grapefruit juice**
   3 **tablespoons lemon juice**
   1 **tablespoon corn starch**
   2 **teaspoons vegetable oil, optional**
   2 **teaspoons honey**
   1 **teaspoon poppy seeds**
   2 **medium cantaloupes**
   2 **cups fresh sliced strawberries**
   2 **cups honeydew melon balls**
      Fresh mint sprigs to garnish

   1. Combine juices, vegetable oil (if desired), and honey in a saucepan. Reserve a few tablespoons of this juice mixture before cooking. Cook remaining juice mixture over medium heat until warmed. Add cornstarch to reserved juice mixture and whisk with a fork until all lumps are dissolved. Add to warmed juice mixture and stir constantly, until thickened and bubbly. Stir in poppy seeds. Cover and chill thoroughly.
   2. Peel cantaloupes, cut each melon into four ¾-inch slices. Place slices on individual salad plates. Combine strawberries and honeydew balls. Spoon ½ cup strawberry/honeydew mixture over each cantaloupe slice. Spoon poppy-seed mixture evenly over fruit. Garnish with fresh mint sprigs.

FRESH FRUIT PLATTER PIE
Serves 8

   1 **Whole-Wheat Cookie Crust (recipe following)**
   ¼ **cup honey**
   3 **tablespoons cornstarch**
   1¼ **cups apple juice**
   1 **teaspoon grated lemon rind**
   2 **tablespoons lemon juice**
   6 **cups assorted fruit, cut in bite-sized pieces (blueberries, kiwi, peaches, raspberries, strawberries, apples, bananas, etc.)**

   1. Prepare Whole-Wheat Cookie Crust (recipe following).
   2. To make glaze: Mix honey and apple juice (reserving ½ cup of juice) in a medium-sized saucepan. Add cornstarch to reserved apple juice and mix together with a fork until cornstarch is dissolved with no lumps. Set aside. Heat apple juice and honey mixture until just before boiling and slowly stir in cornstarch mixture, stirring constantly. Bring to a boil and continue boiling while stirring until glaze becomes clear, about 1 minute.
   3. Remove from heat; stir in lemon rind and lemon juice. Cool to room temperature.
   4. In a large bowl, gently toss the assorted fruit. Pour on the glaze; toss lightly.
   5. Pour the fruit mixture into the Whole Wheat Cookie Crust. Chill 4 hours before serving. Garnish with mint sprigs.

Makes 1 pie.

WHOLE-WHEAT COOKIE PIE CRUST
Serves 8

> 4 **tablespoons margarine**
> 2 **tablespoons honey**
> 1 **egg white, lightly beaten, or ¼ cup tofu, blended smooth**
> ½ **cup whole-wheat flour**
> ½ **cup wheat germ**
> ¼ **cup walnuts or pecans, chopped**
> ¼ **cup shredded unsweetened coconut**
> 1 **teaspoon ground cinnamon or Cinnamon Substitute (see Variations section)**

1. By hand, in a medium-sized bowl, cream the margarine, add the honey and beat in the egg white or tofu.
2. In a separate bowl, mix the flour, wheat germ, nuts, coconut, and cinnamon. Add to the creamed mixture; stir until well blended. (If using a food processor, blend together all step 1 ingredients. Add the remaining ingredients and process until the mixture forms a ball on side of bowl.)
3. Press mixture into a 9-inch pie plate. Bake in a 400° F oven until lightly browned, about 10 minutes. Cool. Use with Fresh Fruit Platter Pie filling.

Makes 1 piecrust.

STRAWBERRY TOFU ICE CREAM
Serves 24

> 2 **pounds (4 cups) soft tofu**
> 1 **cup non-fat milk or soy milk**
> 1 **cup honey or sugar**
> ½ **to 1 cup vegetable oil**
> ¼ **cup fresh lemon juice**
> 2 **20-ounce packages frozen, unsweetened strawberries or other frozen fruit of your choice**
> 2 **tablespoons vanilla**
> ¼ **teaspoon salt**
> **Fresh strawberries to garnish**

1. Blend all ingredients together in a blender until smooth and creamy. (Divide ingredients into smaller parts to accommodate size of blender.)
2. Freeze in an ice-cream maker and serve. Garnish with fresh strawberries.

Makes about 3 quarts.

FRENCH APPLE TART
Serves 8-10

> 6 **tablespoons margarine**
> 1 **cup whole-wheat flour**
> 2 **tablespoons lightly toasted sesame seeds**
> 2½ **tablespoons ground pecans or walnuts**
> 1 **egg white, beaten or ⅛ cup tofu, blended smooth**
> 1 **tablespoon chilled orange juice**
> ½ **cup dried apricots**
> 3 **cups water or apple juice**
> 4 **tablespoons honey, optional (may delete if using apple juice)**
> 5 **large baking apples**

1. To make the crust: Cut margarine into the flour by hand or in a food processor using steel blade. Add toasted sesame seeds. (Toast sesame seeds in dry skillet on medium-high heat just until they begin to pop and lightly brown. Do not overtoast or the flavor changes.) Add pecans or walnuts, and egg white or tofu. Add ½ tablespoon orange juice; mix in more juice if the mixture is too dry to form a ball. Mix all ingredients together with a fork until mixture holds together and forms a ball easily, or process until mixture forms ball (about 30 seconds).
2. Turn mixture out onto work surface. Shape into a ball with your hands. Wrap the ball of crust in plastic wrap and chill for 1 hour while you prepare the glaze.
3. To make glaze: Place the apricots and water or apple juice in a 2-quart saucepan; bring to a boil. Cover and reduce heat, and simmer until apricots are soft, about 12 minutes. (Or microwave by placing apricots and liquid in covered microwave-safe dish and cooking on high for 5 minutes. Change micro-

111

wave setting to low and cook an additional 7-9 minutes, or until soft.) Puree mixture in a food processor or blender. Mix in honey. Allow glaze to cool to room temperature. (Glaze will be thin.)

4. With a rolling pin, roll out dough between 2 sheets of waxed paper. Transfer the dough to a 10- or 11-inch French tart pan (preferably one with a removable bottom). Trim the edges of dough that extend beyond the pan. If the dough accidentally tears, press it back together. (Tart shell may be refrigerated for several days, or frozen for up to 1 month.)

5. Bake tart shell crust in preheated 375° F oven for 15 minutes. After crust cools, either remove crust from the pan to add filling or just leave in the tart pan to serve.

6. To make filling: Slice the apples ¼-inch thick. Steam apples in steam basket over boiling water or microwave in covered dish with 2 teaspoons water until crisp-tender, about 6-8 minutes in steam basket, or 5 minutes on high in microwave. Stir and cook an additional 3-5 minutes. Drain any moisture from apples, reserving liquid. Let apples cool slightly.

7. Arrange the apple slices in a circular pattern over the crust, evenly overlapping edges to add as many slices as possible.

8. Lightly drizzle glaze over apples (thinning glaze slightly with reserved apple water, if necessary) either down the center of the slices, or spread evenly over entire top of apples and crust. Serve tart immediately to prevent soggy bottom crust. This can be further prevented by spreading half of glaze over bottom of crust and arranging apples on top of glaze. Lightly drizzle remaining glaze down the center of apple slices. Serve slightly warm or at room temperature.

Makes one 10- or 11-inch tart.

CAROB-COATED BONBONS
Serves 24-36

  1½ **cups chopped dates**
  1¼ **cups peanut butter**
   1 **cup chopped walnuts or pecans**
  ¾ **cup toasted wheat germ**
   1 **cup coconut flakes**

  ⅓ **cup instant nonfat dry milk or instant tofu or soy milk powder**
  3 **to 4 tablespoons fruit juice or water**
  1 **1-pound package carob chips**
  ¼ **cup hot water**

1. With hands, mix together dates, peanut butter, walnuts or pecans, wheat germ, coconut, instant powdered milk, and 3-4 tablespoons fruit juice or water. Roll into balls.

2. Melt carob chips with water in top of double boiler over hot water. Using tongs, dip candy pieces into carob to cover entire ball. Arrange on waxed paper and store in refrigerator or freezer. (These bonbons also taste great without any carob covering.)

Makes about 3 dozen bonbons.

PEAR SORBET WITH RASPBERRY SAUCE
Serves 6-8

  4 **16-ounce cans sliced or whole unsweetened pears**
    Honey to taste, optional
  1 **10-ounce package frozen raspberries**
    Mint leaves, optional

1. In 3 large (1-gallon) Ziploc bags, arrange pears in single layers. Freeze overnight or until frozen solid.

2. In a food processor or blender, process pears in small batches, until icy smooth. Do not overprocess or pears will melt. (If you prefer a sweetened sorbet, add a small amount of honey to processor while processing pears). Pour puree in dish and store, covered, in freezer until serving time, but do not allow to freeze through. (If sorbet does freeze thoroughly, you will need to break it up and reprocess it in processor.) An alternative for storing sorbet until serving time: place in an ice-cream maker to maintain frozen state. This is especially useful if you're serving a large group.

3. Thaw raspberries by placing package in hot water or in microwave on defrost. Puree raspberries in food processor or blender. Strain pureed raspberries to remove seeds at this point if you wish.

4. To serve; ladle small amount of sauce into serving bowl and place scoops of pear sorbet on the sauce. You may also pour sauce over sorbet. Garnish with mint leaves if desired.

Makes 5¼ cups sorbet and 1⅓ cups sauce.

STRAWBERRY SHORTCAKE
Serves 4

4 **Whole-Wheat Yeast Biscuits (see recipe following)**
1 **cup fresh or frozen raspberries**
2 **tablespoons honey, optional**
½ **teaspoon grated lemon peel, optional**
1 **teaspoon cornstarch**
2 **teaspoons water**
2 to 3 **cups fresh sliced strawberries**
½ to 1 **cup nondairy whipped topping or Nondairy Tofu Whipped Cream (see Variations section)**
Fresh whole strawberries, with stems, to garnish

1. Prepare biscuits (recipe following).
2. Make raspberry puree sauce: Puree raspberries. Strain pureed raspberries to remove seeds. In a small saucepan, combine the strained raspberry puree, honey, and lemon peel, if desired. Stir over low heat until just before boiling. In a cup, combine the cornstarch and water, mixing with fork until dissolved and smooth; add to raspberry mixture, stirring constantly. Cook slowly until thick and smooth. Cover and chill.
3. To serve, place 1 biscuit in serving bowl or plate, either cut in half or left whole. Pour ¼ cup raspberry puree over each biscuit. Top with ½ -¾ cup sliced strawberries and ¼ cup nondairy whipped topping or Nondairy Tofu Whipped Cream. Garnish with fresh whole strawberry. Serve.

Makes 4 strawberry shortcakes.

WHOLE-WHEAT YEAST BISCUITS
Serves 24

½ **cup warm water (110° F)**
1 **tablespoon honey**
1 **package active dry yeast**
1 **cup cornmeal**
1 **cup all-purpose flour**
5 **teaspoons whole wheat gluten flour**
1 **cup whole wheat flour**
½ **teaspoon salt**
1 **cup warm water (110° F)**

1. Sprinkle yeast over ½ cup warm water mixed with honey.
2. Mix cornmeal, flour, and salt in bowl. Add yeast and additional 1 cup warm water to flour mixture and mix well. Place on floured board and knead lightly.
3. Roll out to ½-inch thick, cut with biscuit cutter, place on lightly oiled baking sheet. Cover with towel and place in warm place until doubled in size.
4. Bake in preheated 400° F oven for 15-20 minutes, being careful not to overbake. (Overbaking causes dry and hard biscuits.) Remove from pan and cool on wire rack.
5. To store: seal cooled biscuits in plastic bags.
6. To reheat: Place in paper bag, fold down top and sprinkle outside of bag with water, and reheat in oven at 350° F until warmed through.
7. Serve with strawberry shortcake recipe.

Makes about 24 biscuits.

VARIATIONS

- ▶ Nondairy Cheese
- ▶ Nondairy Milk, Cream, and Sour Cream
- ▶ Nondairy Salad Dressings and Dips
- ▶ Nondairy Mayonnaise
- ▶ Tomato Catsup Without Vinegar
- ▶ Seasoning Substitutes

NONDAIRY PIMENTO CHEESE
Serves 20

- ⅓ **cup cashew nuts**
- ⅔ **cup water, more or less, depending on desired consistency**
- 2 **ounces chopped pimento**
- 1 **teaspoon onion salt**
- 1 **teaspoon garlic powder**
- 1 **teaspoon paprika**
- ¼ **teaspoon savory**
- ⅛ **teaspoon cumin**
- 1 **teaspoon frozen orange juice concentrate**
- 1 **teaspoon lemon juice**
- 1½ **cups cooked garbanzos, millet, or rice**

1. In blender, combine cashews, pimento, seasonings, lemon and orange juice, and ½ cup garbanzos, rice, or millet, Blend with just enough water to allow for blending. Mixture should be smooth and very thick.

2. Add remaining garbanzos, rice, or millet, and just enough water to make of spreading consistency.

3. Refrigerate and use as spread for pizza, pita bread sandwiches, or anytime you would use cheese.

4. To store: This will keep for a week in the refrigerator, or it may be frozen. If you plan to store it longer than one week in the refrigerator, prepare the cooked version below.

5. Tip: You may want to experiment with this recipe's options and versions to find the taste and texture that is just right for you. For example, if you plan to use the cheese as a spread or a dip by itself, rather than in another prepared recipe, such as pizza, you may prefer the texture of the cooked version.

To prepare cooked version:

1. Replace 1½ cups cooked garbanzos, millet, or rice in original recipe with 1 cup uncooked garbanzos that have been soaked for 24 hours.

2. Combine all the other ingredients in a blender. Add soaked, uncooked garbanzos, a few at a time. (This method will give a thicker consistency to the cheese substitute after it is cooked, but either method can be used to prepare the cooked version.)

3. Place in oiled loaf pan and bake at 400° F for 1 hour or until knife may be inserted and come out clean. This will slice nicely or crumble for cheese.

Makes about 2½ cups or 20 2-tablespoon servings.

NONDAIRY TOFU CHEESE
Serves 16

- ½ **cup water**
- 1 **tablespoon tapioca**
- 1 **cup tofu**
- ¼ **cup cashews, rinsed**
- 3 **tablespoons chopped pimentos**
- 3 **tablespoons lemon juice**
- ⅛ **teaspoon dill weed**
- ½ **teaspoon onion powder**
- ½ **teaspoon garlic powder**
- ¾ **teaspoon salt**

Blend all ingredients together until smooth. Cook over medium-low heat, constantly stirring, 5-10 minutes or until tapioca is clear. Chill. Use as spread or dip.

Makes about 2 cups or 16 2-tablespoon servings.

NONDAIRY PARMESAN CHEESE
Serves 16

- ½ **cup yellow flaked food yeast**
- ½ **cup ground sesame seeds**
- 2 **teaspoons garlic powder**
- 1 **teaspoon onion powder**
- 1 **teaspoon chickenlike seasoning, McKay's Chicken-Style Seasoning, or Chicken-like Seasoning (see recipe in seasoning substitutes section)**
- 3 **teaspoons lemon juice**

Combine all ingredients except lemon juice. Place in blender. Add lemon juice and blend until smooth. Store in refrigerator in airtight container.

Makes about 1 cup or 16 1-tablespoon servings.

CASHEW-RICE MILK
Serves 8-10

> ⅔ cup cooked rice, warm
> ½ cup cashews
> 1 teaspoon vanilla (preferably white vanilla)
> ½ teaspoon salt
> 3 to 4 teaspoons honey or 3 to 4 softened dates
> 3 cups water
> 1 banana, optional

1. Place above ingredients in blender and blend until smooth and creamy. (Choose white rice, white vanilla, and honey if color of milk is important. Other ingredients will also make a delicious milk, but it will not be as white in color.)
2. Chill and use in recipes calling for milk.

Makes about 4½ cups or 10 ½-cup servings.

CASHEW-RICE CREAM
Serves 8-12

1. Follow directions for Cashew-Rice Milk, except use only enough water to blend ingredients smooth. Then add more water, a little at a time, until desired consistency is achieved.
2. This can be used in creamy-based soups, gravies, or wherever cream is called for in cooking.

Makes about 2½ cups or 10 ¼-cup servings.

FRUIT CREAM
Serves 4-6

> 1 cup fruit juice, such as unsweetened pineapple or apple juice
> ½ cup cooked cereal (oatmeal, rice, millet, etc.)
> 1 tablespoon nuts or seeds of your choice (cashews, almonds, sunflower seeds, etc.)

1. Using only ½ cup of the juice, blend all ingredients until smooth and creamy. Add remaining juice, a little at a time, until mixture is of desired consistency.
2. Use over hot cereal, waffles, or as a dressing for fruit salad. Serve chilled.

Makes 1½ cups or 6 ¼-cup servings.

NONDAIRY TOFU WHIPPED CREAM
Serves 24

> 1 cup tofu
> 4 tablespoons oil
> 2 tablespoons honey
> ½ teaspoon lemon juice
> ⅛ teaspoon salt
> 1½ teaspoons vanilla (preferably white vanilla)

1. Blend all ingredients in blender until smooth and creamy.
2. Chill and serve as you would whipped cream.

Makes 1½ cups or 24 1-tablespoon servings.

NONDAIRY TOFU SOUR CREAM
Serves 20

> 1 cup tofu
> ¼ cup oil
> 1 tablespoon lemon juice
> 1½ teaspoons honey
> ½ teaspoon salt

Blend all ingredients until smooth and creamy. Use as replacement for sour cream.

Makes 1¼ cups or 20 1-tablespoon servings.

CREAMY BASIL DRESSING OR DIP
Serves 24-32

- 6 tablespoons lemon juice
- 3 tablespoons fresh chopped basil or 1 tablespoon dried basil
- 1 teaspoon dry mustard, optional
- 2 large garlic cloves, minced
- 6 tablespoons olive or safflower oil
- 1½ cups plain low-fat yogurt or 1½ cups tofu
  Salt to taste, optional

Place the lemon juice, basil, mustard, and garlic in a food processor or blender. With the machine running continuously, gradually add the oil, a little at a time. When oil has been completely blended in, add tofu (if desired) and blend until smooth. If using yogurt, gently stir the yogurt into lemon juice mixture. Season with salt to taste if desired. Cover and refrigerate. Stir well before serving. This dressing is most flavorful when allowed to marinate for a day.

Makes 2 cups or 32 1-tablespoon servings.

DILLY DELIGHT DRESSING OR DIP
Serves 20

- 1 cup tofu, mashed
- 2 tablespoons olive or vegetable oil
- 4 teaspoons lemon juice
- ½ to ¾ teaspoon dill weed
- ½ teaspoon salt
- 1 medium garlic clove

Combine all ingredients in blender and blend until smooth and creamy. Chill before serving.

Makes 1¼ cups or 20 1-tablespoon servings.

LEMON-GARLIC DRESSING
Serves 16

- ½ cup olive or vegetable oil
- ½ cup lemon juice
- 2 to 3 garlic cloves, peeled, halved, and speared on toothpick
  Salt to taste, optional

In a small bowl, combine oil, lemon juice, and salt to taste. Drop in the garlic spears. Let stand at room temperature about 1 hour. Remove garlic just prior to serving.

Makes 1 cup or 16 1-tablespoon servings.

HUMMOUS/GARBANZO AND SESAME SEED DIP
Serves 24

- 1 can (15 ounces) garbanzos, drain and reserve liquid
- ¼ cup tahini (sesame paste), or ¼ cup toasted sesame seeds and 2 tablespoons olive oil, blended together in blender to form paste
- 4 tablespoons lemon juice
- 2 large garlic cloves, cut in thirds
- ¼ teaspoon ground cumin
  Salt to taste, optional
  Olive oil or chopped parsley to garnish, optional

Drain garbanzos, reserving liquid. Put garbanzos into a blender or food processor. Add tahini, lemon juice, garlic, cumin, and ¼ cup garbanzo liquid. Blend, adding more garbanzo liquid if needed, until mixture is smooth and the consistency of heavy batter. Season to taste with salt if desired. Serve chilled with drizzled olive oil or sprinkled with parsley.

Makes 1½ cups or 24 1-tablespoon servings.

POPPY SEED DRESSING
Serves 16-32

- ½ **small white onion, chopped**
- ½ **cup honey**
- ⅓ **cup lemon juice**
- 1 **teaspoon dry mustard, optional**
- ¾ **teaspoon salt, optional**
- 1 **cup olive oil or other vegetable oil or ½ cup oil and ½ cup water**
- 2 **tablespoons poppy seeds**

1. In blender or food processor, blend chopped onion on medium speed until onion is slushy.

2. Add honey and lemon juice to onion in blender or food processor. Add dry mustard and salt to taste, if desired.

3. With blender or food processor running on medium-high speed, slowly pour in oil, or oil/water mixture. Mixture in blender will be thick and creamy. If you use oil/water mixture, it will be slightly thinner, but still delicious.

4. Add poppy seeds and blend or process a few seconds longer, being careful to not run too long so that poppy seeds remain whole.

5. Store in refrigerator until needed. Serve chilled with Italian Green Salad or favorite salad combination.

Note: Menu nutrition analysis is based on 2 tablespoons per serving.

Makes 2 cups or 32 1-tablespoon servings or 16 2-tablespoon servings.

TOFU GARBANZO MAYONNAISE
Serves 40-48

- 1 **cup tofu**
- 1 **cup cooked garbanzo beans**
- ½ **cup water**
- ¼ **cup raw cashews, rinsed**
- ⅛ **cup tahini (sesame seed paste) or ¼ cup toasted sesame seeds, blended with 2 tablespoons olive oil to form paste**
- ¼ **cup lemon juice**
- 1 **garlic clove**
- 1½ **teaspoons salt**
- ½ **teaspoon celery seed**
- ½ **teaspoon onion powder**

Blend all above ingredients together in blender until smooth. Use wherever mayonnaise is called for in recipes.

Makes 3 cups or 48 1-tablespoon servings.

CASHEW-RICE MAYONNAISE
Serves 32

- ¼ **cup raw cashew pieces, rinsed**
- 2 **tablespoons lemon juice**
- ⅛ **teaspoon paprika**
- ¾ **cup cooked brown rice, white rice, or millet**
- 1½ **teaspoons orange juice concentrate**
- 1 **garlic clove, cut in thirds**
- 1 **teaspoon onion, minced**
- ¼ **teaspoon dillweed**
- ¾ **teaspoon salt**

Place well-done rice or millet, cashew pieces, and remaining ingredients in blender. Add just enough water to blend very thick and smooth. (Rice or millet must be cooked until well done.) Add water until the mixture is the consistency of mayonnaise. This will thicken as it is refrigerated. Adjust seasonings to your taste.

Makes 2 cups or 32 1-tablespoon servings.

VINEGARLESS TOMATO CATSUP
Serves 32

   2   **cups diced fresh or canned tomatoes**
   1   **4-ounce can tomato paste**
   ½   **red sweet pepper, diced**
   ¼   **cup quartered onions**
   ⅛   **cup frozen orange juice concentrate**
   1   **bay leaf**
   ½   **teaspoon celery seed**
   2   **carrots, cut in chunks**
   ⅛   **cup lemon juice or to taste**
       Salt to taste, optional
       Garlic powder to taste, optional

1. Place all ingredients in blender and blend until smooth and well mixed.
2. Transfer mixture to small saucepan and cook over low heat, stirring constantly until mixture is of desired consistency. The orange and lemon juices give the same tart sweetness as vinegar. Use orange juice and lemon juice to desired taste. This can be frozen, or it can be canned in the pressure cooker according to canning instructions for tomatoes.

Makes about 2 cups or 32 1-tablespoon servings.

CINNAMON SUBSTITUTE

Use coriander seed in equal amounts to cinnamon, or use 1 part coriander seed and 1 part anise seed, or use 3 parts coriander seed and 1 part sweet anise seed. Grind to a powder in an electric Moulinex or by hand with a mortar and pestle. Use in place of cinnamon.

CHILI POWDER SUBSTITUTE

   1   **tablespoon paprika**
   1   **teaspoon cumin**
   2   **bay leaves**
   1   **tablespoon sweet basil**
   1   **tablespoon dried bell pepper**
   1   **tablespoon parsley flakes**
   1   **teaspoon ground dill weed or ½ teaspoon dill seed**
   1   **teaspoon oregano**
   1   **tablespoon onion powder**

Grind all ingredients to fine powder in an electric Moulinex or by hand with mortar and pestle. Store in well-cleaned empty seasoning containers.

Makes about 6 tablespoons or 18 1-teaspoon servings.

CHICKENLIKE SEASONING

   ⅓   **cup yellow flaked food yeast**
   ¾   **teaspoon dried bell pepper**
   ¾   **teaspoon salt**
   ½   **teaspoon celery salt**
   ½   **teaspoon garlic powder**
   1   **teaspoon onion powder**
   ½   **teaspoon sage**
   ½   **teaspoon thyme**
   ¼   **teaspoon marjoram**
   1   **tablespoon parsley flakes**

Mix ingredients and grind to a powder in an electric Moulinex or by hand with mortar and pestle. Store in sealed container.

Makes about ½ cup or 24 1-teaspoon servings.

Alphabetical Index of Recipes

Sectional Index

Complete Nutritional Analysis by Recipe

RECIPE	SERVING	Kcal gm	Pro gm	CHO gm	Fats Total gm	Poly gm	Mono gm	Sat gm	Chol mg	Na mg	Iron mg	Ca mg	Fiber gm	Milk Ex	Veg Ex	Fruit Ex	Bread Ex	Meat Ex	Fat Ex
SPRING MORNING BRUNCH																			
Muesli Cereal	2/3 cup	134.9	3.7	22.9	4.0	0.9	1.8	1.1	0.0	69.4	1.1	28.5	2.6	0.0	0.0	0.8	0.7	0.2	0.8
Potato Chive Squares	3"x4" piece	99.0	4.8	16.6	1.9	1.1	0.4	0.3	0.0	6.4	2.5	49.8	0.8	0.0	0.2	0.0	0.9	0.4	0.2
Garden Patch Yolkless Omelette	1 omelette	267.8	20.9	8.4	16.2	2.6	7.9	4.7	16.2	514.7	1.3	289.8	2.0	0.0	1.2	0.0	0.0	2.5	2.8
Tofu Vegetable Scramble	1 cup	204.6	20.6	8.3	12.1	6.4	4.0	1.7	0.0	31.2	13.9	277.2	0.8	0.0	1.4	0.0	0.0	2.4	1.2
English Muffin Bread	1 slice	76.9	3.0	16.5	0.3	trace	0.0	trace	0.0	107.6	0.9	9.5	2.5	0.0	0.0	0.0	1.0	0.0	0.0
PATIO BRUNCH																			
Strawberry Pecan Belgian Waffles	1 waffle	263.0	8.2	38.3	10.0	4.1	4.0	1.0	0.0	334.9	3.0	54.7	5.0	0.0	0.1	0.4	1.7	0.2	2.2
Strawberry Pecan Oat Bran Waffles	1 waffle	240.4	7.3	34.0	9.1	1.8	4.5	2.0	0.8	275.2	2.4	85.9	3.6	0.2	0.0	0.6	1.3	0.2	2.1
Breakfast Kabobs	1 kabob	79.6	2.8	16.0	1.2	0.5	0.2	0.1	0.0	17.2	1.6	34.8	1.7	0.0	0.6	0.6	0.3	0.0	0.1
Orange Jubilee	8 oz	112.4	3.0	23.3	1.3	trace	trace	trace	0.0	9.4	0.5	20.4	0.3	0.1	0.0	1.5	0.0	0.0	0.2
BRIDAL SHOWER BRUNCH																			
Spinach Cheese Puffs	2 puffs	119.0	8.5	11.3	4.8	0.3	1.5	2.4	13.5	172.0	1.5	206.0	1.3	0.0	0.9	0.0	0.3	1.0	0.6
Tofu Spinach Cheese Puffs	2 puffs	114.9	6.6	14.2	4.4	1.7	1.5	0.7	0.0	97.3	4.8	113.1	1.3	0.0	0.9	0.0	0.6	0.5	0.6
Potato Onion Blintzes Nondairy	1 blintz	129.3	5.4	14.9	5.9	3.0	1.3	0.8	0.0	128.0	2.4	46.5	1.5	0.1	0.3	0.0	0.7	0.3	1.0
Potato Onion Blintzes Dairy	1 blintz	87.4	4.2	13.6	1.9	0.7	0.4	0.4	35.6	37.3	0.5	70.8	1.4	0.2	0.3	0.0	0.7	0.3	0.4
Summer Fruit Ice-Cream Pie	1 piece	305.2	9.3	40.7	13.6	7.2	3.6	1.7	0.0	51.7	4.7	92.6	4.4	0.0	0.3	1.1	0.7	0.7	2.3
Apricot Twist	1 piece	115.5	4.2	23.9	1.7	0.4	0.7	0.2	0.0	85.4	1.5	20.9	2.4	0.0	0.3	0.4	0.7	0.2	0.2
Cinnamon Nut Braid	1 piece	164.7	4.2	23.2	6.9	2.1	3.3	0.9	0.0	120.2	1.4	20.0	2.8	0.0	0.0	0.0	1.0	0.2	1.3
GREEK LUNCHEON																			
Vegetarian Gyro Sandwich	1 gyro	140.3	5.5	20.8	4.9	1.7	1.7	0.7	0.0	207.4	2.6	44.2	4.3	0.0	0.8	0.1	1.0	0.3	0.8
Vegetarian Gyro Sandwich Dairy	1 gyro	128.8	5.9	18.0	4.3	0.2	1.3	2.3	12.7	281.9	1.3	111.1	3.5	0.1	0.7	0.1	0.8	0.3	0.7
Greek Salad	1 cup	53.8	1.4	13.0	3.7	0.4	2.5	0.5	0.0	10.3	0.8	26.3	2.1	0.0	0.9	0.0	0.0	0.0	0.7
Cheese & Garlic Pita Chips	8 chips	61.9	2.4	13.3	0.3	trace	trace	trace	0.0	108.1	0.8	8.4	2.0	0.0	0.1	0.0	0.8	0.0	0.0
BETTER BURGER AND FRIES																			
Garden Nut Burgers Nondairy	1 burger	82.8	5.5	10.0	2.7	1.3	0.6	0.4	0.0	50.3	3.0	61.7	0.5	0.0	0.3	0.0	0.5	0.5	0.3
Garden Nut Burgers Dairy	1 burger	62.9	4.4	9.5	0.8	0.1	0.2	0.2	0.6	118.6	0.5	23.1	0.1	0.0	0.2	0.0	0.5	0.3	0.1
Homemade Whole-Wheat Buns	1 bun	137.4	6.1	27.9	1.1	0.3	trace	trace	0.0	268.3	2.0	17.5	4.2	0.0	0.0	0.0	1.8	0.0	0.0
Fresh Vegetable Basil Soup	1 cup	75.7	3.5	16.1	0.4	0.1	trace	trace	0.0	38.6	1.6	45.0	3.7	0.0	1.2	0.0	0.6	0.0	0.0
Unfried French Fries	3/4 cup	116.0	2.3	27.0	0.1	trace	trace	trace	0.0	7.0	0.4	10.0	1.5	0.0	0.0	0.0	1.6	0.0	0.0
LUNCHEON ON THE MED																			
Falafel	2 falafels	84.5	4.8	10.5	3.3	1.5	0.8	0.4	0.0	50.2	2.2	55.6	2.2	0.0	0.2	0.0	0.6	0.2	0.7
Tahini Dressing Nondairy	1 tbsp	77.4	1.8	2.7	7.1	2.4	3.4	0.9	0.0	1.7	1.5	101.5	1.5	0.0	0.0	0.0	0.0	0.3	1.7
Tahini Dressing Dairy	1 tbsp	81.5	2.3	3.3	7.0	4.2	3.3	0.9	0.1	7.5	1.5	117.0	1.5	0.1	0.0	0.0	0.0	0.3	1.7
Taco From Morocco Nondairy	1 pita sand	258.8	10.5	31.7	11.9	4.2	4.7	1.7	0.0	220.9	5.4	186.5	7.4	0.1	0.6	0.1	1.6	0.6	2.6
Taco From Morocco Dairy	1 pita sand	308.0	16.8	29.6	15.3	4.1	5.4	4.4	16.1	301.8	4.9	376.8	6.6	0.1	0.6	0.0	1.4	1.4	2.9
Tomato Lentil Deluxe Soup	1 cup	156.4	9.2	31.3	0.1	trace	0.2	trace	0.0	40.2	2.5	44.6	6.2	0.0	0.6	0.0	2.0	0.0	0.0
Garlic Flavored Pita Chips	4 lg chips	72.1	3.0	14.0	0.8	0.3	0.2	0.1	0.0	111.0	1.1	21.8	2.2	0.0	0.0	0.0	0.8	0.0	0.1
Hummous Dip	1 tbsp	40.5	1.3	3.9	2.3	0.7	0.9	0.2	0.0	70.9	0.9	37.1	1.3	0.0	0.0	0.0	0.2	0.2	0.5
FINNISH SUMMER DELIGHT																			
Finnish Summer Soup Nondairy	1 cup	180.0	4.7	29.4	5.8	1.1	3.2	1.0	0.0	140.4	1.7	44.1	1.9	0.0	1.1	0.0	1.2	0.3	1.1
Finnish Summer Soup Dairy	1 cup	179.1	8.5	30.6	3.3	0.6	1.7	0.6	2.5	123.6	1.4	224.7	1.4	0.6	1.1	0.0	1.0	0.0	0.6
Sunshine Sandwich Nondairy	1 sandwich	54.2	2.8	8.4	1.5	0.3	0.4	0.1	0.0	106.4	1.1	29.2	2.6	0.0	0.6	0.0	0.4	0.1	0.2
Cheese Delight Sandwich Nondairy	1 sandwich	60.9	2.3	9.9	1.5	0.2	0.4	0.1	0.0	127.5	1.1	24.2	2.1	0.0	0.4	0.0	0.5	0.1	0.2
Cheese Delight Sandwich Dairy	1 sandwich	83.6	5.2	8.7	3.2	0.2	0.9	1.5	8.0	165.1	0.8	111.8	1.7	0.0	0.4	0.0	0.4	0.5	0.4
Apricot Wedges	1" wedge	211.1	3.7	30.6	9.4	2.4	4.4	1.9	0.0	143.9	1.9	24.4	3.8	0.0	0.0	1.3	0.7	0.1	2.0

Diabetic Exchanges

RECIPE	SERVING	Kcal gm	Pro gm	CHO gm	Total gm	Poly gm	Mono gm	Sat gm	Chol mg	Na mg	Iron mg	Ca mg	Fiber gm	Milk Ex	Veg Ex	Fruit Ex	Bread Ex	Meat Ex	Fat Ex
ITALIAN AT ITS BEST																			
Stuffed Mushrooms	1 large	27.2	0.6	2.0	2.0	0.4	1.1	0.3	0.0	31.1	0.4	7.9	0.4	0.0	0.2	0.0	0.0	0.0	0.4
Italian Sauce	1 cup	65.2	2.8	14.6	0.7	0.3	0.1	0.1	0.0	279.5	2.1	65.6	1.4	0.0	2.2	0.0	0.0	0.0	0.2
Pasta Primavera & Italian Sauce	4 cups	214.3	8.2	44.8	1.6	0.2	trace	trace	0.0	61.1	2.6	65.2	5.0	0.0	2.1	0.0	2.3	0.0	0.0
Vegetable Bouquet & Basil Dressing	1 cup	93.0	4.4	8.1	5.7	1.3	3.1	0.8	0.0	17.2	3.1	84.1	2.4	0.0	1.3	0.0	0.8	0.4	0.9
Italian Breadsticks	1 stick	79.7	2.9	12.9	2.3	0.3	1.3	0.3	0.0	201.3	1.1	16.7	1.9	0.0	0.1	0.0	0.8	0.1	0.4
COUNTRY TIME FAMILY SUPPER																			
Vegetable Pot Pie Oil-Free Crust	2 cups	399.0	15.3	66.7	9.4	2.3	4.5	1.3	0.0	539.2	6.6	113.3	5.9	0.0	1.1	0.0	3.6	0.7	1.4
Raspberry Walnut Vegetable Salad	1 cup	65.7	2.6	8.8	3.1	1.9	0.6	0.2	0.0	31.9	1.0	38.9	3.3	0.0	1.3	0.0	0.0	0.2	0.5
Herb Cheese Rosette Rolls	1 roll	78.7	3.1	14.3	1.2	0.4	0.4	0.1	0.0	140.0	1.3	19.9	1.3	0.0	0.0	0.0	0.8	0.1	0.2
DINNER FRESH FROM THE GARDEN																			
Artichokes à la Béarnaise	1 serving	59.8	3.6	7.4	2.5	0.9	1.2	0.3	0.0	95.6	2.2	55.6	2.2	0.0	1.3	0.0	0.0	0.3	0.4
Pineapple Potato Boats Nondairy	1 serving	111.5	3.2	18.1	3.3	1.8	0.7	0.4	0.0	50.1	1.4	26.7	1.9	0.0	0.1	0.0	1.0	0.2	0.5
Pineapple Potato Boats Dairy	1 serving	106.1	2.8	17.7	2.9	0.1	0.8	1.8	9.3	52.6	0.3	15.7	1.9	0.0	0.0	0.0	1.0	0.2	0.5
Vegetable Medley	2 cups	98.5	7.7	14.1	2.9	1.2	0.8	0.4	0.0	23.5	3.0	106.9	4.0	0.0	2.4	0.0	0.0	0.1	0.6
Vegetable Medley Dairy Option	2 cups	86.5	7.9	11.2	2.5	0.3	0.5	1.3	4.9	129.6	1.7	139.3	3.3	0.0	2.4	0.0	0.0	0.4	0.1
Avocado-Almond Salad & Dressing	1 1/2 cups	162.6	5.6	9.7	12.8	4.6	5.8	1.5	0.0	74.5	3.2	93.2	3.4	0.0	0.8	0.0	0.0	0.5	2.8
Avocado-Almond Salad Dairy Option	1 1/2 cups	134.6	4.6	9.7	9.9	2.8	5.2	1.2	0.7	38.4	2.1	93.0	3.4	0.1	0.8	0.1	0.0	0.3	2.3
Dilly Twists	1 twist	71.7	3.0	15.0	0.3	trace	trace	trace	0.0	180.7	1.1	17.1	2.0	0.0	0.1	0.0	0.8	0.0	0.0
LA FIESTA GRANDE																			
Vegetable Nachos Nondairy	1/2 cup	47.3	2.5	7.6	1.3	0.2	0.5	0.2	0.0	59.8	1.1	132.3	2.8	0.0	0.9	0.0	0.1	0.2	0.2
Vegetable Nachos Dairy Option	1/2 cup	93.3	8.5	4.9	4.7	0.2	1.3	2.9	16.2	136.7	0.6	205.7	2.0	0.0	0.8	0.0	0.0	1.0	0.5
Chili-Tomato Sauce	2 tbsp	9.2	2.3	1.8	0.3	0.1	trace	trace	0.0	5.1	1.0	3.7	0.3	0.0	0.6	0.0	0.0	0.0	0.0
Chili Beans	1 cup	45.1	2.3	9.0	0.3	0.1	trace	trace	0.0	81.5	1.0	28.2	1.5	0.0	0.6	0.0	0.4	0.0	0.0
Impossible Taco Pie Nondairy	1-3" piece	180.8	5.4	29.4	5.4	1.6	1.9	0.8	0.0	197.0	2.0	37.9	1.7	0.0	0.8	0.0	1.2	0.4	1.0
Impossible Taco Pie Dairy Option	1-3" piece	182.1	4.6	29.1	5.9	0.5	2.0	2.3	6.4	177.0	1.3	41.0	1.6	0.0	0.7	0.0	1.2	0.4	1.0
Fiesta Ensalada	3/4 cups	33.9	1.3	8.2	0.2	0.1	trace	trace	0.0	5.8	0.8	60.0	2.1	0.0	0.7	0.3	0.0	0.0	0.0
Mexican Rice	1 cup	129.4	2.2	19.2	5.1	3.4	0.5	0.4	0.0	48.3	0.7	22.2	2.8	0.0	0.6	0.0	1.0	0.0	0.9
Guacamole	1 tbsp	41.9	0.6	2.3	3.8	0.4	2.4	0.5	0.0	3.5	0.3	4.3	0.9	0.0	0.1	0.0	0.0	0.0	0.1
Toasted Corn Chips	8 chips	67.2	1.2	12.8	1.1	0.0	0.5	0.0	0.0	53.4	0.5	42.0	1.1	0.0	0.0	0.0	0.8	0.0	0.0
Fiesta Fruit Punch	8 oz	71.7	0.6	18.2	trace	trace	trace	trace	0.0	12.0	0.2	8.8	0.3	0.0	0.0	1.3	0.0	0.0	0.0
ANNIVERSARY DINNER FOR TWO																			
Spinach Lasagne & Italian Sauce	2 pieces	367.2	19.7	54.6	10.5	3.6	3.7	1.3	0.0	250.9	10.2	254.5	3.1	0.0	3.0	0.0	2.3	1.2	1.3
Spinach Lasagne Dairy Option	2 pieces	282.9	17.7	51.4	2.1	0.3	0.2	0.4	2.5	484.3	3.7	160.4	3.1	0.0	2.5	0.0	2.3	1.0	0.1
Vegetable Bundles	1 bundle	12.6	0.7	2.7	trace	trace	trace	trace	0.0	6.0	0.4	13.1	1.0	0.0	0.8	0.0	0.0	0.0	0.0
Italian Salad & Dressing	1 cup	97.2	1.3	8.5	7.0	0.7	5.0	1.0	0.0	58.4	1.0	38.0	1.7	0.0	0.8	0.0	0.0	0.0	1.4
Whole-Wheat Italian Bread	1 slice	93.3	3.4	20.0	0.4	trace	0.0	trace	0.0	134.4	1.0	11.0	2.8	0.0	0.0	0.0	1.2	0.0	0.0
STARS & STRIPES BARBECUE																			
Barbecued Vegetable Kabobs	1 skewer	208.9	3.8	34.4	7.2	0.8	4.9	1.0	0.0	16.1	1.3	30.7	3.7	0.0	1.2	0.0	1.6	0.0	1.4
Stars & Stripes Watermelon	1 cup	80.9	2.6	15.5	1.9	0.6	0.6	0.2	0.0	7.8	1.4	35.0	2.0	0.0	0.1	1.1	0.0	0.2	0.2
Stars & Stripes Watermelon Dairy	1 cup	70.9	1.5	15.8	1.0	0.1	0.4	0.1	0.1	13.6	0.3	32.3	2.3	0.1	1.0	1.1	0.6	0.4	0.1
Macaroni Salad in Tomato Cups	1 tom. cup	110.2	5.6	14.6	3.9	1.2	1.9	0.5	0.0	103.7	2.9	53.8	2.3	0.0	1.0	0.0	0.6	0.4	0.6
Macaroni Salad in Cups Dairy	1 tom. cup	211.6	2.9	13.9	16.8	8.6	4.6	2.4	12.0	138.6	1.0	16.1	2.3	0.0	0.8	0.0	0.6	0.0	3.8
Roasted Corn on the Cob	1 ear	83.0	2.5	19.3	2.4	0.4	0.2	0.2	0.0	13.0	0.4	2.0	6.6	0.0	0.8	0.0	1.3	0.0	0.0
Hot Herbed Garlic Bread	1 slice	114.3	3.8	20.7	2.4	0.2	1.3	0.3	0.0	135.4	1.3	22.1	2.9	0.0	0.0	0.0	1.2	0.1	0.4
Hot Herbed Garlic Bread Dairy	1 slice	115.0	4.0	20.4	2.5	0.2	1.3	0.5	0.9	157.6	1.2	32.8	2.8	0.0	0.0	0.0	1.2	0.1	0.4
Minted Icey Lemonade	8 oz	105.0	0.0	28.0	0.0	0.0	0.0	0.0	0.0	0.0	0.1	2.0	0.0	0.0	0.0	1.9	0.0	0.0	0.0
TAILGATE PICNIC																			
Pita Bread Pizzas Nondairy	1 pizza	91.1	3.4	17.2	1.7	0.2	0.7	0.2	0.0	189.5	1.4	25.0	2.8	0.0	0.3	0.1	0.9	0.1	0.3
Pita Bread Pizzas Dairy Option	1 pizza	147.9	9.8	15.9	5.6	0.2	1.7	3.0	16.2	289.0	1.1	205.6	2.3	0.0	0.3	0.1	0.8	1.0	0.7
Basket of Vegetables	2 1/2 cups	65.6	1.7	14.5	2.0	0.2	trace	0.2	0.0	76.9	1.4	62.9	5.3	0.0	2.5	0.0	0.0	0.0	0.0
Hot Artichoke Dip Nondairy	1 tbsp	33.3	1.0	2.7	2.0	1.0	0.5	0.2	0.0	33.1	1.0	29.1	0.7	0.0	0.3	0.0	0.0	0.1	0.4
Hot Artichoke Dip Dairy Option	1 tbsp	28.7	1.7	1.9	1.1	trace	0.1	0.3	3.1	38.9	0.2	27.4	0.5	0.0	0.3	0.0	0.0	0.1	0.2
Toasted Corn Chips	8 chips	67.2	2.1	12.8	1.1	0.0	0.0	0.0	0.0	53.4	0.5	42.0	1.0	0.0	0.0	0.0	0.8	0.0	0.2

Diabetic Exchanges — nutrient table. Columns grouped: *Fats* (Total, Poly, Mono, Sat) and *Diabetic Exchanges* (Milk, Veg, Fruit, Bread, Meat, Fat).

RECIPE	SERVING	Kcal gm	Pro gm	CHO gm	Fat Total gm	Fat Poly gm	Fat Mono gm	Fat Sat gm	Chol mg	Na mg	Iron mg	Ca mg	Fiber gm	Milk Ex	Veg Ex	Fruit Ex	Bread Ex	Meat Ex	Fat Ex
VALENTINE CANDLELIGHT DINNER																			
Garden Vegetable Crepes Nondairy	3" wedge	158.1	10.0	13.8	8.2	2.9	2.4	1.1	0.0	109.0	5.0	104.2	2.2	0.1	0.7	0.0	0.5	0.7	1.3
Garden Vegetable Crepes Dairy	3" wedge	150.7	11.6	15.7	4.8	1.5	1.7	1.2	4.2	309.2	0.7	166.6	2.2	0.3	0.2	0.0	0.6	0.8	0.7
Tomato & Mushroom Marinated Salad	1 cup	68.3	3.0	7.7	3.9	0.5	2.5	0.5	0.0	40.7	2.3	59.2	3.4	0.0	1.5	0.0	0.0	0.0	0.7
Whole Wheat Crescent Rolls	1 roll	78.4	2.8	13.2	1.8	0.4	0.7	0.3	0.0	14.8	1.0	12.6	1.3	0.0	0.0	0.0	0.8	0.1	0.3
NEW YEAR'S EVE PIZZA PARTY																			
Vegetarian Supreme Pizza Nondairy	1 slice	193.9	8.0	33.6	5.0	0.7	2.3	0.7	0.0	421.3	4.3	103.5	6.9	0.0	2.3	0.0	1.2	0.3	0.8
Vegetarian Supreme Pizza Dairy	1 slice	212.1	12.9	27.5	7.2	0.5	2.6	3.2	16.0	439.7	3.3	271.5	5.3	0.0	2.2	0.0	0.9	1.0	0.9
Tomato & Cheese Pizza Nondairy	1 slice	178.6	6.7	30.6	4.8	0.6	2.3	0.6	0.0	409.4	3.4	71.7	5.5	0.0	1.7	0.0	1.2	0.3	0.8
Tomato & Cheese Pizza Dairy	1 slice	232.8	15.1	24.9	9.3	0.5	3.2	4.6	24.0	493.0	3.4	330.8	3.9	0.0	1.6	0.0	0.9	1.5	1.2
Antipasto Vegie Cups & Dip	1 vegie cup	76.8	3.7	11.1	2.9	0.9	1.2	0.4	0.0	73.5	2.6	57.6	3.6	0.0	1.8	0.0	0.0	0.3	0.4
Specially Seasoned Popcorn	1 1/2 cups	75.9	2.0	8.0	3.8	0.8	2.2	0.6	0.0	45.9	0.5	6.0	0.6	0.0	0.0	0.0	0.5	0.0	0.8
JINGLE BELLS BUFFET																			
Artichoke Nibbles Nondairy	1-1" square	30.8	1.5	3.0	1.7	0.3	0.8	0.2	0.0	29.0	0.8	18.4	0.6	0.0	0.3	0.0	0.1	0.4	0.3
Artichoke Nibbles Dairy Option	1-1" square	51.7	3.1	1.8	3.6	trace	0.5	0.1	0.0	67.4	0.2	75.0	0.4	0.0	0.2	0.0	0.2	0.5	0.5
French Mushroom Tarts Nondairy	1 tart	119.6	4.5	3.8	9.8	4.6	3.1	1.3	0.0	131.1	2.8	55.4	0.5	0.0	0.3	0.0	0.2	0.5	1.7
French Mushroom Tarts Dairy Optionl	tart	83.3	1.8	3.8	6.9	0.7	2.7	3.1	9.2	49.7	0.2	29.6	0.5	0.0	0.1	0.0	0.2	0.1	1.6
Zucchini Bites	1 piece	10.1	0.5	1.7	0.3	trace	0.1	trace	0.0	9.7	0.3	12.0	0.6	0.0	0.0	0.0	0.0	0.0	0.1
Fresh Vegetable Platter	2 cups	70.5	4.2	15.0	0.6	0.2	trace	0.1	0.0	35.7	1.6	67.8	6.1	0.0	2.8	0.0	0.0	0.0	0.0
Avocado-Tomato Dip	1 tbsp	25.9	0.3	1.1	2.5	0.3	1.6	0.4	0.0	1.7	0.2	1.7	0.5	0.0	0.0	0.0	0.0	0.0	0.7
Christmas Fruit Tree	2 cup	117.5	1.4	30.2	0.7	0.1	trace	trace	0.0	8.6	0.5	26.9	3.4	0.0	0.0	2.1	0.0	0.0	0.0
Christmas Cooler	8 oz	110.3	trace	28.3	trace	0.0	0.0	trace	0.0	19.5	0.3	8.0	0.0	0.0	0.0	1.9	0.0	0.0	0.0
Christmas Tree Braid Nondairy	1 slice	57.1	1.8	9.6	1.6	0.3	0.7	0.0	0.0	74.8	0.7	8.9	1.2	0.0	0.5	0.0	0.5	0.0	0.3
Christmas Tree Braid Dairy Option	1 slice	55.5	1.7	9.5	1.4	0.2	0.7	0.2	0.0	77.3	0.4	5.6	1.3	0.0	0.5	0.0	0.5	0.0	0.3
DELIGHTFULLY HEALTHY DESSERTS																			
Frozen Fruit Terrine	1 slice	94.0	0.9	23.8	0.3	trace	trace	trace	0.0	3.0	0.4	20.1	3.7	0.0	0.0	1.0	0.0	0.0	0.0
Berry-Melon Salad	1 serving	80.9	1.5	19.4	0.5	0.1	trace	trace	0.0	15.2	0.4	23.5	1.6	0.0	0.0	1.3	0.0	0.0	0.0
Fresh Fruit Platter Pie	1 piece	266.5	5.2	44.5	9.2	2.7	3.7	1.9	0.0	80.4	1.7	34.5	5.7	0.0	0.0	1.4	0.8	0.1	1.8
Strawberry Tofu Ice Cream	1/2 cup	185.5	7.2	23.5	8.5	5.4	1.3	0.9	0.0	30.4	4.7	92.8	1.1	0.0	0.3	0.7	0.0	0.8	1.3
French Apple Tart	1 piece	198.9	3.6	24.9	10.7	3.2	5.1	1.5	0.0	86.8	1.7	72.9	4.8	0.0	0.0	0.6	0.6	0.2	2.3
Carob Coated Bon Bons Nondairy	1 bon bon	75.3	2.1	15.4	2.6	1.0	0.4	0.7	0.0	3.6	0.6	27.3	1.8	0.0	0.0	0.4	0.4	0.1	0.7
Carob Coated Bon Bons Dairy	1 bon bon	76.4	2.0	15.7	2.5	1.0	0.4	0.7	0.1	6.6	0.6	34.8	1.8	0.0	0.0	0.4	0.4	0.1	0.6
Pear Sorbet with Raspberry Sauce	3/4 cup	90.2	0.7	23.6	0.2	0.1	trace	trace	0.0	9.1	1.3	19.1	1.6	0.0	0.0	1.7	0.0	0.1	0.0
Strawberry Shortcake with Nondairy Tofu Whipped Cream	1 serving	182.0	5.9	25.9	7.1	4.6	1.0	0.7	0.0	71.2	3.2	65.4	3.8	0.0	0.0	0.7	0.8	0.4	1.1
Strawberry Shortcake With Cool Whip Topping	1 serving	119.7	2.8	23.1	2.4	0.3	0.5	1.1	5.7	55.7	1.0	29.7	3.7	0.0	0.0	0.7	0.8	0.0	0.6
Whole Wheat Biscuits	1 biscuit	60.2	1.8	12.7	0.2	trace	0.0	trace	0.0	45.0	0.6	4.5	0.8	0.0	0.0	0.0	0.8	0.0	0.0
VARIATION RECIPES																			
NONDAIRY CHEESES																			
Nondairy Pimento Cheese	2 tbsp	26.9	1.0	3.4	1.1	0.2	0.5	0.2	0.0	56.8	0.5	7.7	0.8	0.0	0.0	0.0	0.1	0.2	0.2
Nondairy Tofu Cheese	2 tbsp	38.2	2.9	2.0	2.4	0.9	0.9	0.4	0.0	103.0	1.8	35.5	0.2	0.0	0.2	0.0	0.0	0.4	0.3
Nondairy Parmesan Cheese	1 tbsp	40.5	2.4	3.0	2.2	1.0	0.8	0.3	0.0	10.2	1.4	53.6	0.7	0.0	0.0	0.0	0.0	0.1	0.6
NONDAIRY MILK & CREAM																			
Cashew-Rice Milk	1/2 cup	60.7	1.3	7.2	3.2	0.5	1.8	0.6	0.0	108.0	0.5	5.3	0.6	0.0	0.0	0.0	0.2	0.3	0.6
Cashew-Rice Cream	1/4 cup	50.6	1.1	6.0	2.6	0.4	1.5	0.5	0.0	90.1	0.4	4.4	0.5	0.0	0.0	0.0	0.2	0.3	0.5
Fruit Cream	1/4 cup	46.1	0.6	9.3	0.7	0.2	0.5	trace	0.0	1.8	0.4	8.0	0.4	0.0	0.0	0.3	0.3	0.1	0.1
Nondairy Tofu Whipped Cream	1 tbsp	40.8	1.7	1.9	3.2	2.2	0.5	0.3	0.0	12.6	1.1	21.7	trace	0.0	0.1	0.0	0.0	0.2	0.5
Nondairy Tofu Sour Cream	1 tbsp	44.2	2.0	1.0	3.8	2.2	0.9	0.5	0.0	55.0	1.3	26.2	trace	0.0	0.1	0.0	0.0	0.3	0.6
NONDAIRY SALAD DRESSING & DIPS																			
Creamy Basil Dressing & Dip	1 tbsp	42.1	2.0	1.1	3.6	0.8	2.1	0.5	0.0	1.7	1.4	33.7	trace	0.0	0.1	0.0	0.0	0.2	0.6
Poppy Seed Dressing	1 tbsp	78.5	trace	4.7	6.8	0.6	5.0	0.9	0.0	50.4	trace	3.8	trace	0.0	0.0	0.0	0.0	0.0	1.4
Dilly Delight Dressing & Dip	1 tbsp	31.3	2.0	0.8	2.4	0.7	1.2	0.9	0.0	55.1	1.3	27.1	trace	0.0	0.1	0.0	0.0	0.3	0.4
Lemon-Garlic Dressing	1 tbsp	62.3	trace	0.8	6.7	0.6	4.9	0.9	0.0	trace	trace	1.5	trace	0.0	0.0	0.0	0.0	0.0	1.4
Humus/Garbanzo & Sesame Seed Dip	1 tbsp	64.9	2.2	6.3	3.8	1.1	1.6	0.4	0.0	114.0	1.4	59.2	2.1	0.0	0.9	0.0	0.3	0.3	0.8
Tofu Garbanzo Mayonnaise	1 tbsp	25.1	1.2	1.1	1.9	0.6	0.9	0.2	0.0	72.3	0.8	24.3	0.3	0.0	0.0	0.0	0.1	0.3	0.4
Cashew-Rice Mayonnaise	1 tbsp	12.4	0.3	1.7	0.5	trace	0.3	trace	0.0	50.2	0.1	1.8	0.2	0.0	0.0	0.0	0.0	0.2	0.1
Vinegarless Tomato Catsup	1 tbsp	6.2	0.2	1.4	trace	trace	trace	trace	0.0	18.4	0.2	4.5	0.1	0.0	0.2	0.0	0.1	0.0	0.0